200
CLASSIC
SAUCES

Also by Tom Bridge

The People of Bolton on Cookery
The Golden Age of Cookery
Lancashire Recipes Old and New
The Outdoor Cookbook
The History of Lancashire Cookery
Dr William Kitchiner, A Regency Eccentric

200
CLASSIC
SAUCES

GUARANTEED RECIPES
FOR EVERY OCCASION

TOM BRIDGE

BROCKHAMPTON PRESS
LONDON

First published in the UK 1995 by
Cassell
Wellington House
125 Strand
London
WC2R 0BB

This edition published 1998 by Brockhampton Press.
a member of Hodder Headline PLC Group

ISBN 1 86019 8562

Designed by Rowan Seymour
Illustrations by Diane Fisher

Typeset by Keystroke, Jacaranda Lodge, Wolverhampton

Printed at Oriental Press, Dubai, U.A.E.

Contents

Acknowledgements 7
Introduction 9

Basic Ingredients and Techniques 13
Making Basic Sauces 19
Classic French Sauces 31
International and Modern Sauces 59
Dessert Sauces 99

Useful Terms and Techniques 111
Useful Herbs and Spices 113
Further Reading 116
Index of Sauces 119
General Index 123

*I dedicate this book to
Silvino and Adrienne Trompetto*

Acknowledgements

I would like to thank Andy Brittan for all his patience; Beverly LeBlanc, my editor; John Warmisham of the Yang Sing Restaurant in Manchester; Francis Carroll of the Brasserie St Pierre, also in Manchester; Colin Cooper-English, for his welcome advice; Sue Webb of McNeill's Fine Food; and Jeremy Rata of Rookery Hall in Nantwich, Cheshire.

Also my sincere thanks go to Adrienne Trompetto, Jane Thorne, Lucinda Buxton, Rosemary Ashbee and Pam Carter at the Savoy; Julian Groom at the Cavendish Hotel, Jermyn Street, London; Peter Pugson; Lee Bridge Cognetta; Doreen and Shirley Morton, the Gaylord Indian Restaurant, Manchester; the Royal Hotel, Bray, Co. Wicklow, Eire; Antonio Carluccio for our long discussion about sauces; Francis Coulson, the Sharrow Bay Country House Hotel, Ullswater, Cumbria, for not decrying the word 'gravy' and for giving the world Icky Sticky Toffee Pudding; and Susan and Ed Guinan and everyone at Transmedia UK. Finally, many thanks to my wife Jayne for putting up with my late nights over the past three years.

Introduction

Sauce cookery in a small household is very different in scale from the activity that takes place in the restaurants, hotels and grand private establishments where I have worked as a professional chef. Because sauces cooked for domestic use are always made fresh and in small quantities, I have had to convert and test every one of my standard recipes. The result, I believe, makes this book the first collection of classical sauces for the average household.

I've worked with many famous chefs throughout my career, and the one subject we have all agreed upon is that sauces are the soul of food. I have studied in every area of cookery, and the area in which I excelled and enjoyed working the most was the sauce section. When I was training to be a chef, the work with sauces was the most important part of a long and rewarding apprenticeship. I never regret the split shifts of 15-hour days I spent learning the art of sauce-making in restaurants around the world.

My enthusiasm was noticed by a most respected chef, who often said I should share my knowledge and love of sauces. With him in mind, I decided to write about the most popular sauces used in today's kitchens. The food historian in me, however, simply couldn't resist including old English and classic French sauces, which are renowned around the world, as well as an international collection of contemporary recipes, which are simply taken for granted by today's cooks but are well worth having.

Sauce-making is a very important aspect of cookery. Sauces enhance food and can make or break an otherwise perfect recipe. They are quite simply the most talked about aspect of cookery, so they must always be perfect. Too much salt, for example, and they will be ruined, so always allow the person tasting the sauce to add the salt themselves.

Three of the greatest British cooks who wrote on the elaborate subject of sauces were Dr William Kitchiner, MD (1775–1827), author of *The Cook's Oracle* (1817); Yorkshire-born Elizabeth Raffald (1733–81), author of *The Experienced English Housekeeper* (1769); and Silvino Trompetto, *maître-chef de cuisine* at London's Savoy Hotel from 1965 to 1983. Their methods have been copied by numerous writers, chefs and cooks throughout the world.

Some of the best known French chefs who have also made their mark on the sauce world are Jean Anthelme Brillat-Savarin (1755–1826), Antonin Carême (1784–1833), Urban Dubois (1818–1901), the great Auguste Escoffier (1847–1935) and Raymond Oliver, who once said there was little to be said about the English mint sauce and then proceeded to write two pages on it!

As well as providing the basic methods for making classic sauces, the book is enriched with stories about their history that I have compiled from my extensive collection of cookery books. I have included recipes for popular modern variations, herb butters and dips, and I have also described my method of including vinegar in sauces.

You will see that most of the recipes include vinegar, which I consider very relevant in the cooking process. After several years of experimentation, I find that the flavour of even a small amount of vinegar brings out and enhances the particular taste of each sauce. Vinegar tenderizes the surface of the meat and fish, and its acid modifies the surface of proteins, allowing the sauce to penetrate the food. I never use malt vinegar – except on my chips! I am very fortunate that I am able to buy an outstanding brand of flavoured vinegar, but I appreciate that not everybody can pop into London's finest food halls, so I have included recipes on pages 14–16 for the most exciting flavours.

It is very important that you read the basic recipes in the first chapter before you go on to use the other recipes. These tell you how to make basic stocks, which are so important in all cookery, especially sauce-making. Without good stock, your sauces will taste very bland. All good chefs and cooks throughout the world know that a good foundation stock can make or break the flavour of a sauce.

If you are concerned about the high amount of saturated fats traditionally included in sauces, or simply want to lose weight by keeping to a daily calorie allowance, you don't have to abandon the pleasure of eating sauces. Just replace double cream with Greek yogurt, and the butter with polyunsaturated sunflower margarine. You can also substitute a reduced-sodium product for salt, or a commercial sweetener for sugar. When making a cheese sauce, replace the traditional hard cheese, such as Cheddar, with Edam, feta or Brie because these have a lower fat content. Or use one of the reduced-fat soft cheeses sold in supermarkets. You can further reduce the fat content by substituting semi-skimmed milk for whole milk.

Making sauces with these substitutes will, of course, affect the flavour, but it does mean you eat less fat without being deprived of enjoying these wonderful sauces.

For the vegetarian, sauces open up a complete wonderland. Simply substitute vegetable stock for the meat, chicken and fish stock in recipes, and create a vegetarian sauce to complement your favourite dishes.

Cookery writer André Simon wrote in *Basic English Fare* (1960): 'A good cook is like a good actor; you cannot expect good cooking, any more than good acting, without a measure of applause.' I thought of this when Dame Barbara Cartland told me that there are more good chefs in France than in England. I do not agree with the lady, but it is true that there are many more people in France who take an intelligent interest in what they eat and drink, and whose taste is more highly trained and whose critical appreciation is more articulate than those of the British. We still have too many unenlightened people in Britain who claim that they don't mind what they eat. I hope this book helps to inspire an appreciation of good food, especially an appreciation of good English food.

Two people have had a great influence on my career. The first was Silvino Trompetto, MBE, a dear friend and mentor whom I met in 1977 when I was involved in a royal dinner at the National Liberal Club. Sadly, Tromps, as he was affectionately known to his friends, died on 25 August 1993. He was the last of the great British chefs of the old school, and the first British chef to be awarded the MBE. Tromps was also very dismissive of the myth that French chefs were the best in the world. Born in London in 1920 to Italian parents, he was educated at Salesian College, Battersea, in the classical tradition. At the age of four Tromps fell on a metal bucket, almost severing his nose, and during the next eight years he underwent a series of operations at Guy's Hospital under the supervision of Sir Harold Gillies. Fortunately, the accident did not affect his sense of smell, and by the age of 18 he became a chef under Oddenino, who ran a restaurant training school in London.

Tromps later joined the Dorchester Hotel, in London, as acting *sous-chef*, and by 1946 he was head chef at the Grand Hotel in Brighton. From there, he became head chef and director of the Albany Club in Savile Row, where the food has an excellent reputation all round the world. Finally, in 1954, Tromps went to the Savoy as *premier sous-chef*, where he rapidly ascended the hierarchy. On Auguste Laplanche's retirement in 1965, Tromps became the first non-Frenchman to hold the position of *maître-chef de cuisine*. I often asked Tromps to write his memoirs, but he would just grin and say he had started them! Trompetto's fame very quickly spread. Pope Paul VI summoned him to the Vatican for a special audience in 1973 because he was first 'Italian' head chef at the Savoy, and a year later he received the MBE for his services to the catering industry.

I often discussed sauces with Tromps and he would listen with close attention whenever I talked about my methods and ideas. During a dinner in 1986 he said: 'Tom, I've known several chefs who love their job and were trained to be chefs, but you have been born with this gift.'

Peter Pugson, a close friend, defined the special qualities of Tromps when he wrote: 'Now he is gone; but great men by their nature are not missed: their greatness is like a lighthouse, a gleaming legacy to guide all who follow. No one who works with or for me will ever go away without some of this great man's teaching being inherited by them.'

The second person who was such an influence on my life was cookery writer Michael Smith. This man was the finest gentlemen, with a heart of gold and wonderful energy. He was an indefatigable promoter of British food throughout the world.

He was a Yorkshireman whose achievements in cookery writing, combined with his appearances on the BBC's *Pebble Mill at One*, made him a household name. I consider him to have been the complete ambassador on the history of British food and drink.

As well as his appearances on daytime television, Michael worked behind the scenes of the television productions of *The Duchess of Duke Street* and *Upstairs Downstairs* for the BBC, where his vast knowledge was essential in accurately portraying England's culinary history. As *The Duchess of Duke Street* was based on one of my favourite personalities, Rosa Lewis of the Cavendish Hotel, in London's Jermyn Street, he invited me to the set, a kindness I greatly appreciated.

His enthusiasm never waned. It seemed that whenever we spoke, Michael was happily quoting from *The Encyclopaedia of British Food* or telling me about a forgotten English recipe he was determined to revive. I hope that my attempts to continue his work are a fitting tribute to him.

Basic Ingredients and Techniques

Herbs and Spices

Excellent herbs had our fathers of old
Excellent herbs to ease their pain
Alexanders and Marigolds,
Eyebright, Orris and Elecampane
Basil, Rocket, Valerian, Rue,
Verbain, Dittany, Call-me-to-you-
Cowslip, Melilot, Rose of the Sun.
Anything green that grew out of mould
Was an excellent herb to our fathers of old.

RUDYARD KIPLING

I have been a chef for thirty years, and at the beginning of my career, as a *commis chef* in Manchester, there was a great deal controversy among cookery writers about herbs, about which I knew little. I thought that thyme and sage came out of what Fanny Cradock described as 'those dreadful packets of dried herbs whose flavour dominates any dish'.

But British chefs weren't always so hesitant about seasoning their cooking with herbs and spices. I spend a great deal of time reading antique cookery books, and as early as the 14th century British chefs were adding more spices and native herbs to add to their sauces than their French counterparts, resulting in fascinating variations on recipes. Here are two example I would like to share with you.

Sauce cameline, for example, was served with meat, and a 1375 recipe from French royal chef Guillaume Tisel (1326–95), more commonly

known as Taillevent, contained ginger, mace, cinnamon, cloves, pepper, vinegar, grain of paradise (cardamom) and was thickened with bread, rather than flour, which hadn't yet become the fashion. The English version, on the other hand, contained ginger, cloves, cinnamon, currants, nuts and vinegar and used bread-crumbs as the thickening agent. The *sauce verde* recipe in one of my very old French cookery books includes parsley, ginger, vinegar and bread, while on the English side of the channel it was more flavourful, containing the same basic four ingredients as well as mint, garlic, thyme, sage and cinnamon.

I think it is interesting to see how English chefs were using garlic in this recipe, while their French counterparts weren't, and that vinegar was a common ingredient in both countries.

In the past thirty years, herbs have become regular ingredients in most cookery generally and sauce-making specifically. I use a variety of herbs throughout this book, all of which are not readily available at supermarkets. I consider mint to be the essential herb in English cookery. New potatoes and peas are boiled with it; it is added to pea soup and is essential for mint sauce. The French scorn this most English of sauces, but then probably they have only ever had the English hotel version – bits of dried mint floating in a sea of cheap malt vinegar. Made with lavish amounts of finely chopped fresh garden mint mixed with sugar and a little hot water and wine vinegar, however, it becomes the most wonderful accompaniment to spring lamb.

Some herbs are so seldom needed that they can be replaced quite easily by another. I think there is a great deal of fun to be had blending and varying the herbs that you are using in a special dish, and letting your friends and guests guess what ingredients give the dish its unique flavour and charm. You will realize as you read through this book that working as a development chef has encouraged me to bend the rules and dare to experiment.

Herbs have been used in cookery for thousands of years, and since many of the plants have such a short growing season, it has always been necessary to preserve their leaves and seeds, usually by drying. To dry herbs, gather them in the morning, tie them into small bunches and hang them, head down, somewhere there is a slight draught. After a few days, when they are really crisp, break the bunches down and pack them into clean, air-tight jars.

Some of my favourite herbs and spices are listed on pages 113–16.

Vinegars

The use of vinegar as a seasoning for foodstuffs has an honoured place in the story of human diet, according to the *Larousse Gastronomique*:

> In Greek and Roman antiquity, the words *oxybaphon* and *acetabulum* were the names for bowls that were placed, filled with vinegar, on the dining table, for guests to dip their bread in.
>
> In the 13th century, among the street vendors who had the right to cry their wares in Paris, some rolled a barrel in the street, announcing to the hoteliers and housewives: *Vinaigres bons et biaux! Vinaigre de moutarde i ail!* (Good and beautiful vinegars! Mustard and garlic vinegar!)

Raymond Oliver, whose work I admire, said: 'Its use in cookery stimulates the appetite. It ages well and is easy to prepare. It is the unquestioned ally of preservation. It has an aseptic action. It enjoys sunlight, rose petals, benjamin, cinnamon and tarragon. It settles down happily with red cabbage and gherkins.'

As you read through this book, it should become apparent that I also consider vinegar to be an essential ingredient in sauce-making. The most elaborate vinegar, the most sophisticated, the most subtle, such as rose petal, saffron or bergamot vinegars, bring out the unsuspected qualities in many sauces. The examples that illustrate this the best are devilled sauce (page 37), Robert sauce (page 56), Béarnaise sauce (page 32) and my recipe for rose petal and honey sauce (page 73).

Sue Webb, a good friend of mine, works with vinegars every day in her family's cottage industry producing McNeill's Fine Food in Oxfordshire. She is without doubt one of the leading authorities on the subject at present working in Great Britain, and her rose petal, tarragon, orange and green peppercorn, English herb and citrus vinegars are my favourites. I spent four years developing sauce recipes that incorporate my vinegar method and having tried many French vinegars, I am very proud to say we do have the finest vinegars in the world on our own shores.

Sue's vinegars are sold in Harrods and Fortnum & Mason, in London, but I realize that if you are reading this in Australia or South Africa, or even in Aberdeen, it's going to be a bit difficult to pop out and pick up a bottle, so I have devised recipes for these delicious vinegars. As well as being an important ingredient in many of my sauce recipes, I'm sure you'll enjoy using these in salad dressings.

Good quality vinegar should be transparent and clear. When you bottle vinegar, it is important that you use warm, clean bottles that can be sealed air-tight with a vinegar-proof cork or a plastic lid. Also, make sure you use non-metallic sieves and spoons while you are making the sauces that contain vinegar. If vinegar comes into contact with metal it causes a chemical reaction that taints the flavour.

Raspberry Vinegar

Use this method to make any fruit-flavoured vinegar, such as strawberry, blackberry or blackcurrant, by simply substituting your favourite fruit for the raspberries. All fruit vinegars should be allowed to stand for at least four days and stirred twice a day before they are bottled. Then leave the bottles to stand in a cool, dark and dry place for at least two weeks before you use the vinegar so the flavour matures. *Makes about 1 litre/1¼ pints.*

  450g/1lb raspberries, hulled and rinsed
  600ml/1 pint red wine vinegar
  450g/1lb sugar

Put the raspberries in a large non-metallic bowl and pour over the red wine vinegar. Gently stir together, then cover the bowl with a tea towel and leave the mixture to stand at room temperature for 4 days, stirring at least twice daily with a wooden spoon.

Pass the vinegar through a fine non-metallic sieve into a saucepan. Add the sugar and stir until it dissolves, then bring the mixture to the boil, stirring. Lower the heat and allow the mixture to simmer for 10 minutes.

Pour the vinegar into warm bottles and close with non-metallic lids. Leave to mature for at least 2 weeks before using. If you store this in a cool dry place, it should keep for at least 8 months.

VARIATIONS

Honey and Caper Vinegar Use 450g/1lb capers, 450g/1lb clear honey and 600ml/1 pint white wine vinegar. Use the same method as for raspberry vinegar, adding the honey instead of the sugar. When you bottle the vinegar, add 8 capers to each bottle.

Lemon Vinegar Use 450g/1lb sliced lemons and 600ml/1 pint white wine or distilled vinegar. Use the same method as for raspberry vinegar but do not add any sugar. Bring to the boil, then simmer for an additional 10 minutes. Leave to stand for 4 days, covered with a tea towel, and stir twice a day. Pour into bottles and add fresh lemon slices, then close with non-metallic lids. Leave to mature as for raspberry vinegar.

Lemon and Black Peppercorn Vinegar Use 100g/4oz dried black peppercorns for each 600ml/1 pint white wine or distilled vinegar. Use the same method as for lemon vinegar (above). When you bottle the vinegar, add 1 tablespoon peppercorns and 1 tablespoon shredded lemon rind to each bottle.

Orange and Green Peppercorn Vinegar Use 100g/4oz dried green peppercorns for each 600ml/1 pint white wine or distilled vinegar. Use the same method as for lemon vinegar (above). When you bottle the vinegar, add 1 tablespoon peppercorns and 1 tablespoon shredded orange rind to each bottle.

Rose Petal Vinegar

My favourite vinegar! I must confess, however, that not even I can claim to make this to the standard of McNeill's here in England. It can be costly to make this in small quantities but I guarantee nothing can replace it in the devilled sauce (page 37) or rose petal and honey sauce (page 73) recipes. It is also wonderful to use in salad dressings and creamy sauces. Use rose petals that are all the same colour and ones that haven't been sprayed with pesticides. *Makes about 600ml/1 pint.*

175g/6oz fresh rose petals
600ml/1 pint white wine or distilled vinegar

Place the rose petals in a large non-metallic bowl and pour over the vinegar. Gently stir together, then cover with a tea towel and transfer the bowl to a dark cupboard to prevent any loss of colour, which is so important. Leave for at least 2 weeks but not longer than 4 weeks; do not stir during this time.

Pass the vinegar through a fine non-metallic sieve. Pour the vinegar into dry but warm bottles and add about 6 fresh petals to each, then close with non-metallic lids. Leave to mature in a cool, dark and dry place for at least 4–6 weeks before using. If tightly sealed, this will keep for up to a year in a cool, dark and dry place.

VARIATION

Herb Vinegars Prepare as for rose petal vinegar but substitute 450g/1lb fresh herbs for the rose petals. Be sure to pick the herbs in the morning and just before they flower for the best flavour. Pick the whole stalk, not just the leaves. After the vinegar is strained, add a few fresh sprigs to each bottle.

Cooking with Oils

Several types of oil are used in cookery, and most of them are obtained from the seeds of plants – rape, soya, cotton, sunflower, groundnut, coconut, palm, sesame, maize, poppy and olive, for example. Groundnut or peanut oil is a clear oil, extracted from peanuts, and it is often used in wok cookery, when it can be mixed with flavoured oils such as sesame oil. Cottonseed oil is purified and used as the basis of vegetable cooking fats.

The most often used oils, at least in kitchens in Britain, are sunflower oil and rapeseed oil, but my own preference is for olive oil, and when a recipe includes olive oil, please do not try to substitute it, as some chefs I know do, with cooking oil. This ruins the flavour of the sauce and is a complete waste of time and effort.

Olive oil has been used in Spain, Greece, Italy and Portugal for thousands of years, but in Britain we have only been weaned away from butter and other animal fats in the last twenty years or so by chefs who have advocated the use of vegetable oils – especially sunflower, rapeseed and olive oils – and by the discovery that these oils, especially olive oil, are far better for your health.

Olive oil is the basic ingredient of most cold sauces, as butter is of hot sauces. It combines a beautiful bland oiliness with – if you use a first pressing or virgin oil – a delightful flavour. Extra virgin olive oil, which is green and has an extra-strong flavour, is made from the first cold pressing of selected olives. Virgin olive oil is more refined than extra virgin, and it is excellent for fish and game sauces. Ordinary olive oil is even more refined but is less expensive than extra virgin and virgin oils. After butter, it is the most widely used ingredient in Europe.

Olive oil tends to go cloudy and streaky when it is cold, so do not keep it in your refrigerator or in a chilly place in winter. If the oil does turn cloudy, however, do not worry – its quality will not have been affected and it will readily turn clear again as soon as it returns to a warmer temperature.

French cooks often use walnut and grapeseed oils, which, like sesame oil, are best used for cooking rather than for sauce making. They also preserve goat's milk cheeses in virgin olive oil, to which are added sprigs of fresh thyme, rosemary and bay leaves. The resulting liquor is then used for making mayonnaise and vinaigrette dressings.

Oils are also used to good effect in marinades, and the marinade is then often used in the making of a sauce. Most often these marinades are used in barbecue cookery and for game, because not only do they help to break down the fatty tissues in meat but also to preserve the meat.

When it comes to cooking oil I have several preferences. Most often, I use corn or rapeseed oils, but I also like to cook with olive oil, walnut oil and sesame oil. In recipes that just specify 'cooking oil' you can use the flavoured oil you like best.

Garlic Oil

I make my own garlic oil by adding 6 cloves of peeled garlic to 500ml/¾ pint pure olive oil. This should be left for at least 2 months before use.

Tom's Brittany Sauce Vinaigrette

This is a typical sauce vinaigrette, which was always served to me during the hot summer months when I was paying homage to the restaurants of Brittany.

Always keep some of this sauce ready to hand. You can keep it in a large screw-topped jar in your refrigerator. *Makes about 600ml/1 pint.*

> 75g/3oz Dijon or French mustard
> pinch of salt
> freshly milled black pepper
> 150ml/5fl oz tarragon vinegar
> 1 teaspoon freshly chopped parsley
> 5 shallots, peeled and finely chopped
> 3 garlic cloves, peeled and crushed
> 1 sprig of thyme
> 250ml/8fl oz walnut oil
> 150ml/5fl oz virgin olive oil
> 4 white peppercorns

Put the mustard, salt, pepper, vinegar and parsley into a bowl and blend. Add all the remain ingredients and blend thoroughly.

Pour into a large storage jar, chill for 2 hours and shake before using.

Mock Smoked Salmon

The Brittany sauce vinaigrette is an excellent summer sauce to serve with this very quick and simple recipe, made with fresh salmon and smoked haddock.

> 4 salmon fillets, each 175g/6oz
> 4 finnan haddock fillets, each 50g/2 oz
> 150ml/5fl oz sauce vinaigrette
> 1 lime, sliced

From the centre of each salmon fillet, make a thin slice, outwards to each side. Fold out the sides and season with 2 tablespoons of the sauce vinaigrette.

Place a finnan haddock fillet into the centre of a salmon fillet and fold over the sides of the salmon, to cover the haddock. Wrap the fillets in kitchen film and leave to stand for 24 hours.

Still with the fillets wrapped in kitchen film, poach lightly for 15 minutes in a steamer. Place the fish on a serving dish, adding the remaining sauce vinaigrette and garnishing with slices of lime. The marinade helps the finnan haddock to smoke the salmon.

Making Basic Sauces

Stock is simply the flavoured liquid made by simmering fish, poultry, meat or vegetables, and it almost always includes bones. The slow, gentle cooking process draws out the flavour and colour of the ingredients and the collagen from the bones, which gives stock body and causes it to cool with a jelly-like texture. It is these characteristics that will enhance both the flavour and appearance of any sauce you make with the stock.

Making Stocks

Whatever sauce you are making, it will taste best if the base is a home-made stock, rather than a stock cube. I don't like to use stock cubes, but I recognize that many people do so to save time, as some stocks will take up to four hours to simmer, while a cube only takes only a minute to dissolve. Yet, I can only emphasis that the flavour from a stock cube really does nothing for the flavour of a sauce. The taste of a sauce made with a stock cube will be similar to any other sauce made with a cube because they contain the same ingredients. A home-made stock is far superior, as it adds its fresh, unique flavour from a selection of ingredients, and you know exactly what has gone into the finished sauce.

If you are using stock cubes, however, their flavour can be improved if you simmer the dissolved cube for a few minutes with meat trimmings, fish bones or heads, or vegetables. But I have to say, this is not the way to my heart. When you are preparing a fresh stock be sure to include any scraps of fish and meat, poultry carcasses, bones and vegetable trimmings that would otherwise be thrown away. Do not include poultry skin, however, as it is far too pungent and fatty.

Fish Stock

When you are preparing fish, do not throw away any fish heads, skins or trimmings because these are what give a fish stock its flavour and body. Monkfish, turbot, whiting and sole bones are especially good to use, but you can also use bones from any inexpensive white fish. Do not use oily fish, however, such as mackerel or herrings, because of the large amount of oil they contain.

You will see I have not included any salt in the recipe because some fish are naturally salty, so extra salt would ruin the flavour of the stock. I also use a combination of whole peppercorns and freshly milled pepper in this and my other stock recipes, depending on how much pepper flavour I want.

Keep fresh fish stock refrigerated and use within 48 hours or freeze for up to 7 days. *Makes about 1.8 litres/3 pints.*

1.8kg/4lb fish bones and trimmings
50g/2oz butter
225g/8oz onion, finely chopped
225g/8oz leek, finely chopped
225g/8oz celery, finely chopped
3 tablespoons lemon juice
8 black peppercorns
1 bay leaf
sprig of fresh parsley
150ml/5fl oz dry white wine
4 tablespoons white wine vinegar
1.8 litres/3 pints water

Thoroughly rinse and chop up the fish bones. Melt the butter in a large saucepan over a low heat, then add the onion, leek and celery and sauté for 3 minutes until they are slightly softened.

Add the fish bones and trimmings along with all the remaining ingredients, except the water, and simmer for about 8 minutes until the wine is slightly reduced.

Add the water and slowly bring the mixture to the boil, skimming the surface as necessary, then lower the heat and simmer, uncovered, for 30 minutes.

Pass the stock through a fine non-metallic sieve and leave it to cool for 1 hour so the flavours have time to blend. It is then ready to use or refrigerate.

Court Bouillon

Use this herb- and vegetable-flavoured basic stock for poaching fish as it imparts a unique flavour, especially if you use it with salmon. You can freeze this in small portions so it is ready when you need fish stock for poaching fish or to add flavour to fish sauces. *Makes about 1.2 litres/2 pints.*

2 litres/3½ pints water
600ml/1 pint dry white wine
100g/4oz carrots, finely chopped
100g/4oz leek, finely chopped
100g/4oz onion or shallots, finely chopped
1 celery stick, finely chopped
sprig each of fresh dill, thyme and rosemary
1 garlic clove
1 bay leaf
8 white peppercorns
4 tablespoons white wine vinegar
4 coriander seeds

In a very large saucepan over a high heat, bring the water and white wine to the boil. Add all the remaining ingredients, lower the heat and simmer for 15 minutes, skimming the surface as necessary.

Leave the stock to stand for at least 2 hours to allow the flavours to blend before you poach any fish in it.

Meat Stock

As you progress through this book, I hope you will appreciate that each sauce possesses a distinct flavour and character of its own, and this is the sauce used to give flavour to many of the sauces intended to be served with meat. This is also the base of Espagnole sauce (pages 38–9), which, in turn, becomes the base for many other sauces. *Makes about 1 litre/1¾ pints.*

450g/1lb beef bones, chopped
450g/1lb shin of beef, chopped
50g/2oz beef dripping
2 leeks, sliced
2 large carrots, sliced
1 large onion, sliced
1 celery stick, sliced
4 white peppercorns
4 tablespoons white wine vinegar
2 bouquet garnis
sprig of fresh thyme
salt and freshly milled black pepper

Preheat the oven to 220°C/425°F/gas mark 7. While the oven is heating, blanch the bones in a large saucepan of boiling water for 10 minutes. Drain them well, then put them in a roasting tin with the shin of beef and beef dripping and roast in the centre of the oven for 40 minutes.

Transfer the bones to a large, deep flame-proof casserole or heavy based saucepan over a high heat. Add the leeks, carrots, onion, celery, peppercorns, vinegar, bouquet garnis, thyme, salt and pepper and enough water to cover. Bring the mixture slowly to the boil, skimming the surface as necessary. Cover the casserole or pan with a tight-fitting lid, lower the heat and simmer the stock over the lowest possible heat for 3 hours to extract all the flavour from the bones and vegetables. Top up with hot water if the level of liquid falls below the solid ingredients.

Pass the stock through a fine non-metallic sieve into a large bowl. Leave the stock to settle for 5 minutes, then remove the fat from the surface by drawing absorbent kitchen towels over it. Adjust the seasoning if necessary and leave to stand for at least 2 hours for the flavours to blend. If not using immediately, cover and refrigerate for up to 7 days. Meat stock can also be frozen for up to 2 months.

Veal Stock

Use the same ingredients and method as for making meat stock (above), but substitute 2.7kg/6lb veal knuckle bones and fresh veal (combined weight), for the beef bones and shin of beef. After the stock has simmered, pass it through a fine non-metallic sieve and leave it to cool for at least 2 hours so the flavours blend. If not using immediately, cover and refrigerate for up to 7 days. Veal stock can also be frozen for up to 3 months. *Makes about 1 litre/1¾ pints.*

Chicken Stock

Use raw chicken trimmings, giblets, feet and the carcass, but do not include any skin because it is too greasy and pungent. If you are not going to use this immediately, refrigerate it in a covered container for up to 7 days, or freeze it for up to 3 months. *Makes about 1 litre/1¾ pints.*

chicken trimmings
1 onion, chopped
1 leek, chopped
1 bay leaf
4 tablespoons white wine vinegar
1.8 litres/3 pints water
salt and freshly milled black pepper

Put the chicken trimmings, onion, leek, bay leaf, vinegar and water in a very large saucepan over a high heat and bring to the boil, skimming the surface as necessary. Lower the heat and leave to simmer for 3 hours, skimming the surface every 15 minutes.

Pass the stock through a fine non-metallic sieve. Taste and adjust the seasoning. Leave to cool for at least 2 hours before using so the flavours have time to blend.

Game Stock

This is a two-stage stock that you begin by using the same ingredients and method as for making chicken stock (page 21), but substituting the bones and trimmings from any game for the chicken trimmings and bones.

After you have made the basic game stock, enrich it by adding 150ml/5fl oz veal stock (page 21) with 6 juniper berries and 4 tablespoons red wine vinegar, a sprig of fresh thyme and a little sprig of rosemary.

Bring to the boil, then lower the heat and simmer for 1 hour. Pass through a fine non-metallic sieve. Leave to cool, then cover and refrigerate for up to 4 days if it is not to be used immediately. Game stock can also be frozen for up to 3 months. *Makes about 1 litre/1¼ pints.*

Vegetable Stock

Use large pieces of fresh, clean vegetables, and do not include cabbage, cauliflower or brussels sprouts; they give off a very distinctive taste and smell that will overwhelm the other flavours. Use 8 shallots, 3 sticks celery, 2 carrots, 2 leeks, 2 onions, 1 swede, 1 parsnip and 1 turnip.

Put the chopped vegetables in a large saucepan over a high heat, add 4 tablespoons white wine vinegar and about 2 litres/3½ pints water. Bring to the boil, then lower the heat and simmer for 1 hour, skimming the surface as necessary. Season well. Pass through a fine non-metallic sieve. Leave to cool for at least 1 hour so the flavours have time to blend, then cover and refrigerate for up to 3 days if not using immediately. Vegetable stock can be frozen for up to 3 months. *Makes about 1 litre/1¼ pints.*

The Importance of Roux in Classic Sauce Making

A roux is simply a cooked mixture of flour and butter that thickens and give body to sauces when it is combined with the liquid. Many sauces start by making a roux in the saucepan, or you can take a tip from professional kitchens and have a large amount of roux ready in the fridge as I do. (I think all cooks should have a batch of roux along with Espagnole sauce (pages 38–9) and a selection of flavoured vinegars (pages 14–16) at hand when preparing to make sauces.)

You will see in the following recipes that the longer a roux is cooked the darker it becomes, which will determine the colour of the sauce.

White Roux

Use this method every time a roux is required. I always make up 450g/1lb roux at a time, as whatever I am not using immediately will keep for up to three weeks in a covered container in the refrigerator. *Makes about 450g/1lb.*

225g/8oz unsalted butter
225g/8oz plain flour

Melt the butter in the saucepan over a low heat, then stir in the flour and cook, stirring occasionally to prevent the mixture from browning. After about 12 minutes, when the mixture becomes light in colour and crumbly, take the pan off the heat and allow the roux to cool completely.

Spoon the roux into a screw-top jar, cover and refrigerate until required.

VARIATIONS

Blond Roux Use the same ingredients and method as for the white roux, but cook for about 15 minutes until the roux develops the faintest tint of colouring. Use this when making a tomato sauce.

Brown Roux This is cooked in the same manner as the white and blond roux, however, the butter should be replaced with good-quality beef dripping and the weight of flour should be increased to 300g/10oz. Cook the roux for about 17 minutes until it is a light chocolate brown colour. Use this for making meat sauces and soups.

Sauce for Veal

As you read through this book, you'll see I have often included rose petal vinegar in my recipes. (See page 16 for recipe.) Yet this recipe is one of the many old ones that illustrates how long this delicious vinegar has been a feature of English cooking. When you are cooking, remember that no spice should overpower another flavouring; spices are used to make a fresh flavour. It is in this that a good cook has scope to display genius.

This may be made with water in which carrots have been cooked, and can be flavoured with quinces, cooked to a pulp, and crab apple juice. To this should be added a little claret, sugar, lemon juice, nutmeg, pepper, salt, rose petal vinegar and a little ground clove.

Useful Sauce-making Advice

• Always use a large heavy based saucepan with a well-fitting lid when making sauces. If you can afford a copper saucepan, I recommend you use that because it conducts the heat evenly. I also recommend you use a wooden spoon for stirring because a metal spoon can give off a metallic taste when it comes into contact with a metal pan.

• To remove all fat from the surface of a sauce, turn off the heat and sprinkle a few drops of cold water over. This causes the fat to rise so that it can be easily spooned off.

• When raw egg yolks are included in a hot sauce, make the sauce in a double boiler, or a heatproof bowl set over a pan of simmering water, to prevent the yolks becoming so hot that they scramble or curdle. Also to prevent the sauce curdling, the yolks should be beaten with a small amount of cold water, then they can be whisked with a small amount of the hot hot sauce before they are added to all the sauce mixture a little bit at a time, whisking until the sauce is smooth. Return the sauce to the heat and stir all the time with a wooden spoon until the sauce thickens. It is very important that hot sauces are never brought to the boil or they may curdle.

• Always remember that extra seasoning does not improve a sauce. It can ruin the taste. Always remember to taste before you season. It is important that the final seasoning should be done by the person eating the sauce. (These are points so charmingly made by Dr William Kitchiner on pages 42–3.)

What to Do If a Sauce Goes Wrong

No matter how carefully you follow a recipe, there is always the possibility that the consistency will not be quite right, so here are my failproof tips for fixing sauces:

• To get the lumps out of a sauce, beat thoroughly with a whisk, then strain through a fine non-metallic sieve into another saucepan.

• If the sauce is too thin, mix 1 tablespoon sifted plain flour with 2 tablespoons cold water to make a smooth paste. Gradually whisk the paste into the sauce over a low to medium heat, whisking constantly, until the sauce thickens.

• If the sauce is too thick, stir in a little more of the stock or other liquid used in the sauce.

• To prevent a skin forming on a savoury sauce, place a piece of buttered grease-proof paper or cling film lightly over the surface.

Basic Sauces

White Sauce

This is a versatile sauce that can easily be flavoured and that has many uses in modern kitchens. The actual flavour of a white sauce depends on the added ingredients, such as parsley, anchovies, herbs or mushrooms, as you can see from the numerous variations. *Makes about 300ml/10fl oz.*

2 tablespoons white roux (page 23)
300ml/10fl oz milk, warm
pinch each of grated nutmeg and dry thyme
2 tablespoons white wine vinegar
salt and freshly milled white pepper
3 tablespoons double cream

Put the roux into a saucepan over a medium heat and heat slowly, stirring constantly, until it softens. Slowly stir in the milk until the sauce is very smooth, then continue simmering for 4 minutes, stirring occasionally.

Add the nutmeg, thyme, vinegar, salt and white pepper and simmer for just a few minutes. Stir in the double cream, blending very slowly for a light, smooth texture. Taste and adjust the seasoning.

VARIATIONS

Anchovy Sauce Use the method and ingredients above but substitute 300ml/10fl oz warm fish stock (pages 19–20) for the milk and add 2 teaspoons anchovy essence and 1 teaspoon lemon vinegar with the other flavourings.

Caper Sauce Use fish stock (pages 19–20) or meat stock (pages 20–21) instead of milk, depending on whether you are going to serve this with fish or meat. Add 2 tablespoons capers and 2 tablespoons honey and caper vinegar (page 15). I serve this with halibut, swordfish, red mullet or salmon.

Herb Sauce Stir in 2 tablespoons finely chopped fresh herbs, selecting the herbs to complement the fish, meat, poultry or vegetables the sauce is to be served with. (See the herb butters on page 30.) Always use fresh herbs, and do not re-heat the sauce after the herbs have been added. Serve this with all root vegetables, as well as trout, bream and oysters.

Mornay Sauce Stir 75g/3oz grated cheese, 4 tablespoons double cream, 1 teaspoon dry English mustard and freshly milled white pepper into the hot white sauce. Serve this with fish and vegetables.

Mushroom Sauce Instead of starting with the roux, melt 15g/½oz butter in a saucepan, add 50g/2oz finely chopped mushrooms and fry until they are softened. Stir in the 1 tablespoon plain flour and proceed with the recipe, using 150ml/5fl oz milk and 150ml/5fl oz vegetable stock (page 22). Use oyster mushrooms and add 4 tablespoons mushroom ketchup for added flavour. This sauce goes particularly well with lamb cutlets and veal or pork steaks.

Onion or Shallot Sauce Use the same method as for making the mushroom sauce, cooking 1 finely chopped large onion or 8 finely chopped shallots in the butter. Season the sauce well with salt and freshly milled black pepper.

Parsley Sauce Stir 2 tablespoons finely chopped fresh parsley to the hot basic white sauce. Serve with ham, fish, chicken or vegetables.

Rich Cheese Sauce Stir 50g/2oz grated Cheddar cheese and 50g/2oz grated Lancashire cheese with 1 teaspoon prepared English mustard and 2 tablespoons soured cream into the hot sauce. Use this sauce to make Welsh rarebit: stir a little stout or beer into the sauce, then pour the sauce over slices of toast, sprinkle each slice with

1 tablespoon grated cheese and grill until golden brown and bubbling. You can also use this recipe to make cauliflower cheese, sprinkled with fresh breadcrumbs. For **Italian Rich Cheese Sauce**, replace the cheese in rich cheese sauce with 100g/4oz freshly grated Parmesan cheese.

Shrimp Sauce Stir 100g/4oz cooked peeled shrimps or prawns, a dash of anchovy essence, 1 tablespoon tomato sauce and a few drops of lemon vinegar into the hot sauce. Serve with fresh fish or your favourite seafood recipes. It is also a good sauce to serve in vol-au-vents with sliced lobster tail as a first course.

White Fish Sauce Use the same method as for making shrimp sauce (above), but replace the milk with 150ml/5fl oz fish stock (pages 19–20). To make a simple supper, place fish fillets of your choice in an ovenproof dish, pour over the sauce and bake at 200°C/400°F/gas mark 6 for 20–25 minutes until the fish is cooked through and flakes easily.

Béchamel Sauce

This classic variation of white sauce was named in honour of the vain, mean and rather negative character of Louis de Béchamel, Marquis de Nointel, Lord Steward of the Household of the Court of Louis XIV of France. *Makes about 300ml/10fl oz.*

15g/½oz butter
2 tablespoons chopped onion
1 tablespoon plain flour
300ml/10fl oz milk, warm
2 sprigs of fresh parsley
5 white peppercorns
pinch each of grated nutmeg and dry thyme
2 tablespoons white wine vinegar
3 tablespoons double cream
salt and freshly milled white pepper

Melt the butter in a saucepan over a medium heat, add the onion and fry until softened. Stir in the flour and cook for about 2 minutes. Slowly stir in the milk until the sauce is very smooth, then continue simmering for 4 minutes, stirring occasionally.

Add the parsley, peppercorns, nutmeg, thyme, vinegar, salt and milled white pepper and simmer for just a few minutes. Stir in the double cream, blending slowly for a light, smooth texture. Pass the sauce through a fine non-metallic sieve. Taste and adjust the seasoning.

Velouté Sauce

This is a basic white sauce made with stock, rather than milk, and a blond roux (page 23). If, for example, you are making a sauce to serve with chicken breasts, use a chicken stock; for fish dishes, use fish stock.

This sauce can be made ahead and stored in the refrigerator for up to two days. Do not freeze it. *Makes about 300ml/10fl oz.*

100g/4oz butter
8 shallots, thinly sliced
100g/4oz plain flour, seasoned with salt, sifted
1 litre/1¾ pints meat, chicken or fish stock (pages 19–20), boiling
4 tablespoons single cream
25g/1oz mushroom stalks
pinch of coarsely crushed black peppercorns
grated nutmeg

Melt the butter in a saucepan over a medium heat, add the shallots and fry, stirring occasionally, until they are softened but not coloured. Stir in the flour and cook, stirring frequently, being careful not to allow the flour to colour.

Add the boiling stock and cream, stirring constantly. Add the mushroom stalks, crushed peppercorns and grated nutmeg and allow the stock to simmer for 35 minutes.

Pass the stock through a fine sieve.

VARIATIONS

Sauce Allemande also called **sauce parisienne**. The French can be very confusing when they name sauces, often giving the same sauce two names, which is what has happened with this example. Velouté sauce becomes this sauce when you add egg yolks to it; the more yolks you add, the thicker the sauce will be. To thin the sauce, keep adding cream.

Breton Sauce Add 50g/2oz each finely shredded leek, finely shredded celery heart, chopped onion, thinly sliced mushrooms, 50g/2oz butter, 150ml/5fl oz white wine and 150ml/5fl oz double cream to 60ml/2fl oz fish, chicken or meat stock to velouté sauce,

Chaudfroid Sauce Dissolve 4 leaves gelatine or 1 teaspoon powdered gelatine and add it to 50ml/2fl oz velouté sauce. This is used warm to coat and decorate canapés and other food for a buffet presentation.

Chivry Sauce Add 1 tablespoon finely chopped fresh chervil and tarragon to 150ml/5fl oz velouté sauce made with chicken or fish stock.

Diplomat Sauce Add 50g/2oz lobster butter (page 30), a pinch of cayenne pepper and 2 tablespoons brandy to Normandy sauce (below).

Mushroom Sauce Cook 100g/4oz sliced button mushrooms in the butter with the shallots, then continue with the main recipe.

Normandy Sauce Add 4 tablespoons mushroom sauce, 6 tablespoons oyster juice blended with 2 egg yolks and 150ml/5fl oz double cream to 50ml/2fl oz fish velouté sauce. If you also add a sliced truffle soaked in a little Madeira, the sauce becomes *sauce Lagupière*

Sauce Ravigote (hot) Season 300ml/10fl oz chicken velouté sauce with 3 tablespoons tarragon vinegar, 1 tablespoon chopped fresh tarragon, ¼ teaspoon dry thyme and a bay leaf. Stir in 6 sautéed chopped shallots and 2 sautéed chopped garlic cloves.

Sauce Riche Add 75g/3oz lobster meat to diplomat sauce (above).

Sauce Talleyrande Simmer a chicken velouté sauce with 50g/2oz mirepoix of vegetables, 50g/2oz finely diced tongue and 25g/1oz finely diced truffles that have been sautéed with 4 tablespoons Madeira. Strain and stir in 100ml/4fl oz double cream. Serve this with chicken, duckling, pork or veal.

Bercy Sauce

During several discussions with Silvino Trompetto (page 11) we talked about the importance of this velouté-based sauce. Too many cooks and chefs serve sauces like this that overpower the accompanying fish dishes, and we both agreed that this needs to be flavoured with great care. So if you want extra strength in the flavour, I suggest you use white wine vinegar in place of white wine and add 50g/2 oz thinly sliced white leek with the shallots.

Bercy sauce is served most frequently with fish, so I've given the recipe with fish stock and fish velouté sauce, but if you want to serve it with fish chicken or beef, substitute the relevant stock and velouté sauce.

I cannot emphasize too strongly, and I may repeat myself, but it is essential to use good quality wine in sauce-making. I know it is only a matter of taste, but the correct wine really does make a difference to a sauce, so please do not use cheap 'plonk' as some hotels and restaurants do today. Food and wine writer André Simon always insisted that cooks should use only the best wines, and I agree that the quality of wine really does make a difference to the flavour, bouquet and colour of any sauce. *Makes about 300ml/10fl oz.*

175ml/6fl oz melted clarified butter

6 shallots, finely chopped

150ml/5fl oz dry white wine, such as Chardonnay

150ml/5fl oz fish stock (pages 19–20)

300ml/10fl oz fish velouté sauce (page 26)

1 tablespoon chopped fresh parsley

Put 50ml/2fl oz of the clarified butter in a saucepan over a medium heat, add the shallots and cook for 3 minutes, stirring frequently. Add the white wine and fish stock and boil until the liquids are reduced by one-third. Stir in the velouté sauce and bring to the boil, then lower the heat and simmer for 5 minutes.

Remove the pan from the heat and slowly whisk in the remaining clarified butter and the parsley.

Melted Butter Sauces

Dr William Kitchiner on the subject of butter sauces from *The Cook's Oracle* (1817):

Is so simple and easy to prepare, that it is a matter of general surprise, that what is done so often in every English kitchen, is so seldom done right. Foreigners may well say, that although we have only ONE SAUCE for Vegetables, Fish, Flesh, Fowl, &c. – we hardly ever make that good.

It is spoiled nine times out of ten, more from Idleness than from Ignorance, and rather because Cook won't than she can't do it, – which can only be the case when Housekeepers will not allow Butter to do it with.

GOOD MELTED BUTTER cannot be made with mere flour and water; there must be a full and proper proportion of Butter. As it must always on the Table, and is THE FOUNDATION OF ALMOST ALL OUR ENGLISH SAUCES; we have Melted Butter and Oysters,

Parsley,

Anchovies,

Eggs,

Shrimps,

Lobsters,

Capers, &c.&c.&c.

I have tried every way of making it; and I trust, at last, that I have written a receipt, which if the Cook will carefully observe, she will constantly succeed in giving satisfaction.

In the quantities of the various Sauces I have ordered, I have had in view the providing for a Family of half-a-dozen moderate people.

Never pour Sauce over Meat, or even put it into the dish;– however well made, some of the Company may have an antipathy to it;– Tastes are as different as Faces: moreover, if it is sent up separate in a boat, it will keep hot longer, and what is left may be put by for another time, or used for another purpose.

Parsley and Butter Sauce

In French cookery books, this is recognized as 'Melted Butter, English Fashion', or ' Dutch sauce' when diced lemon, a little ground allspice and vinegar are added. This was Henry VIII's favourite sauce, which he would have enjoyed most when poured over fricassee of rabbit.

The recipe in Kitchiner's *The Cook's Oracle* reads:

Wash some Parsley very clean, and pick it carefully leaf by leaf;

Put a tea-spoonful of salt into half a pint of boiling water: boil the parsley about ten minutes; drain it on a sieve; mince it quite fine, and then bruise it into pulp.

The delicacy and excellence of this elegant and innocent Relish depends upon the Parsley being minced very fine: put it into a sauce-boat, and mix with it, by degrees, about half a pint of good melted butter – only do not put so much flour to it, as the Parsley and Butter over boiled things, but send it up in a Boat.

Butter Sauce

I serve this rich, simple sauce with broccoli, mange tout and asparagus, as well as halibut and shark and tuna steaks. *Makes about 100ml/4fl oz.*

    75g/3oz butter
    1 egg yolk
    1 tablespoon water

Melt the butter in a saucepan over a medium heat. Beat the egg yolk with the water and blend into the melted butter. Serve immediately.

VARIATIONS
Beurre Noir also known as black butter sauce. Melt 100g/4oz best quality unsalted butter, then add 1 tablespoon chopped fresh parsley, 1 teaspoon well-drained capers and 2 tablespoons white wine vinegar. Serve with fish and eggs.

Beurre Noisette Melt 100g/4oz best quality unsalted butter, then add 2 tablespoons lemon juice. Serve with grilled or lightly poached fish.

Egg Sauce Add 2 finely chopped hard-boiled eggs and 2 tablespoons finely snipped fresh chives to the butter sauce. Serve with salmon steaks or root vegetables.

Mustard Sauce Stir 1 teaspoon English mustard blended with 1 tablespoon sherry vinegar into the butter sauce. For a coarse grain sauce, use a coarse grain mustard. Serve with lamb or veal.

Sauce Polonaise Toast 50g/2oz breadcrumbs under a hot grill. Melt the butter and sauté 1 tablespoon finely chopped shallots, then add the breadcrumbs with 1 chopped hard-boiled egg. Use as a topping for cauliflower or other vegetables.

Beurre Blanc

Also known as white butter sauce, this classic French sauce is served with white fish and many vegetarian dishes. *Makes about 100ml/4fl oz.*

    75g/3oz shallots, finely chopped
    100ml/4fl oz good quality white wine, such as
        Chardonnay
    50ml/2fl oz white wine vinegar
    1 bay leaf
    8 black peppercorns, crushed
    pinch of salt
    250g/9oz best quality unsalted butter, diced

Put the shallots, white wine, vinegar, bay leaf and black peppercorns and salt in a saucepan over a high heat and bring to the boil. Continue to boil until the liquid is reduced to about 50ml/2fl oz. Strain the liquid through a fine non-metallic sieve, then return it to the pan.

Over a very low heat, whisk in the butter, piece by piece, whisking until the sauce forms.

Savoury and Herb Butters

These butters are handy to have in the freezer, ready to be sliced and added to hot food. Each of these should be chilled before you use it. If you are not using it immediately, however, it will keep for several weeks in the fridge if it is well wrapped and can be frozen for up to six months. Use 100g/4oz softened best quality butter for each of these recipes:

Garlic Butter Pound the butter with 2 finely chopped garlic cloves and a little finely chopped fresh parsley, then season with freshly milled black pepper and a pinch of salt. Serve with grilled or baked meat, fish or poultry. This is also a splendid topping for a jacket potato.

Lobster or Shrimp Butter Pound 3 tablespoons cooked and finely chopped lobster tails or shrimps with the butter, then add 1 teaspoon anchovy paste, a little lemon juice and a pinch of cayenne pepper. Serve this sauce with your favourite fish.

Maître d'Hôtel Cream the butter until it is soft and smooth, then add 1 tablespoon finely chopped fresh parsley and 1 teaspoon lemon juice. Season with freshly milled black pepper and salt. Serve with fish, chicken or steaks.

Watercress or Parsley Butter Cream the butter until soft and smooth, then add 2 tablespoons finely chopped fresh parsley or watercress. Serve with meat, fish or vegetables.

Tromp's Lobster Butter

This is the finishing touch for Silvino Trompetto's wonderful lobster sauce on pages 53–4. Blend the crushed lobster coral in a pestle and mortar with 1 crumbled bay leaf and a pinch of dried thyme. Add 4 tablespoons softened best quality butter and 2 sautéed finely chopped shallots and combine well, then rub through a fine sieve.

Make the mixture into a sausage shape, wrap it in foil and place it in the freezer for at least 30 minutes. To serve, slice very thinly and interleaf with thin lemon slices on top of the hot dish.

Herb Butters

Use the following as a guide for making your own flavoured butters to serve with game, meat, poultry and seafood.

Beef Basil, chervil, fennel, sweet marjoram, oregano, parsley, rosemary, tarragon and thyme.

Chicken Chervil, chives, dill, sweet marjoram, parsley, oregano, sage, tarragon and thyme.

Fish Basil, chervil, dill, fennel, sweet marjoram, oregano, parsley, rosemary, tarragon and thyme.

Game Basil, chervil, fennel, dill, marjoram, oregano, parsley, rosemary, sage, tarragon and thyme.

Lamb Basil, chives, dill, sweet marjoram, mint (wild), spearmint, rosemary, tarragon and thyme.

Pork Basil, dill, fennel, marjoram, oregano, parsley, rosemary, sage, tarragon and thyme.

Shellfish Basil, chervil, chives, dill, oregano, parsley, rosemary and thyme.

Classic French Sauces

Egg Sauces

To my mind Hollandaise sauce, Béarnaise sauce and mayonnaise are the tastiest sauces, and I think this view is supported in their popularity throughout the world.

I suggest you use a double boiler when making Hollandaise, Béarnaise and Bavarois sauces, because it cooks the ingredients more gently than if they are put over direct heat, so there is less chance of the eggs curdling. If you do not have a double boiler, use a heatproof bowl set over a saucepan of gently simmering water. Make sure that the bottom of the bowl does not touch the water, or the eggs will curdle.

Hollandaise Sauce

If this delicate sauce does curdle while you are making it, you can bring it back to a homogeneous thickness by beating a fresh egg yolk in another pan and then very slowly whisking in the curdled mixture. *Makes about 225ml / 8fl oz.*

  1 tablespoon white wine vinegar
  6 black peppercorns
  1 tablespoon water
  4 egg yolks
  200ml / 7fl oz melted clarified butter
  1 tablespoon lemon juice
  cayenne pepper
  pinch of salt

Put the vinegar, peppercorns and water in a small saucepan over a high heat and boil until the liquids are reduced by half. Remove the pan from the heat and allow to cool a little.

Whisk the egg yolks and reduction together in the top of a double boiler over simmering water, or in a heatproof bowl that will fit over the pan with plenty of room underneath. Put warm water into the pan, then place the basin in the pan, making sure the bottom does not touch the water. Whisk in the clarified butter, little by little, whisking constantly for 12–15 minutes until the sauce thickens. Add the lemon juice and cayenne, then pass the sauce through a fine non-metallic sieve. Taste and adjust the seasoning. Serve with lightly steamed asparagus, artichokes, broccoli, stuffed eggs or fresh fish.

VARIATIONS

Maltaise Sauce Add the grated rind of 1 large orange and 1 teaspoon Curaçao or other orange-flavoured liqueur to the completed sauce. Serve with duckling and game.

Mild Mustard Sauce Stir 2 tablespoons Dijon mustard into the finished sauce. Serve with steaks and chicken.

Mousseline Sauce Just before serving fold 150ml / 5fl oz whipped double cream into the sauce.

Rich Mousseline Sauce Make up the Hollandaise sauce and stir in 50g/2oz finely grated Lancashire or Cheddar cheese, then fold in 150ml/5fl oz whipped cream. Sprinkle with some finely chopped fresh dill. This sauce goes quite well with cauliflower.

Bavarois Sauce

The unique flavour in this comes from the crayfish butter – *beurre d'écrevisses* – which is messy to make but can only be described as tremendous tasting. You need to pulverise the crayfish or lobster shells, then simmer them in 450ml/15fl oz clarified butter for 20 minutes. Remove the pan from the heat and allow the butter to cool, then pass it through a fine sieve.

If you do find this too time consuming, however, you can substitute potted shrimp, available from fishmongers and good supermarkets. This sauce is excellent with barbecued king prawns or baked crayfish tails. *Makes about 225ml/8 fl oz.*

> 300ml/10fl oz white wine vinegar
> sprig of fresh thyme
> 1 bay leaf
> 1 teaspoon chopped fresh parsley
> 6 black peppercorns, crushed
> 1 teaspoon grated horseradish
> 4 egg yolks
> 100ml/4fl oz melted clarified butter
> pinch of grated nutmeg
> salt and freshly milled black pepper
> 50g/2oz crayfish or potted shrimp butter
>   (see page 30), melted
> 2 tablespoons double cream, whipped

Put the vinegar, thyme, bay leaf, parsley, peppercorns and horseradish in a small saucepan over a high heat and boil until the vinegar is reduced by half. Remove the pan from the heat and allow the mixture to cool.

Whisk the egg yolks and the reduction together in the top of a double boiler over simmering water, or in a heatproof bowl that will fit over a saucepan with plenty of room underneath. Put warm water into the pan, then place the basin in the pan, making sure that the bottom does not touch the water. Add a pinch of salt and whisk in the clarified butter, little by little, whisking constantly until the sauce thickens. Season with nutmeg, salt and pepper.

Pass through a fine non-metallic strainer and finish off the sauce by stirring in the crayfish or potted shrimp butter and folding in the whipped cream.

VARIATION

Lobster Newburg Sauce Add 3 tablespoons dry sherry, 3 tablespoons double cream, a generous pinch of paprika and freshly milled white pepper. Serve with boiled lobster or other seafood.

Béarnaise Sauce

This is said to be the creation of the *chef des cuisines* of the Pavilion Henri IV at Saint-Germain-en-Laye, near Paris, and dates from about 1800. Care and a very light-hearted attitude must be taken when making this sauce; it must be loved and cosseted and only freshly picked herbs used to achieve the correct subtle flavouring. This recipe first appeared in print in 1818 in *La Cuisinière des Villes et des Campagnes* by Louis Eustache Audot.

This sauce should never be allowed to get really hot, and it is served lukewarm; never re-heat it. Serve with medium-rare fillet steak (*chateaubriand*), sirloin steak or lightly cooked fish. In the late 19th century this sauce was known as *sauce chateaubriand* as it was a traditional accompaniment to the steak. *Makes about 250ml/9fl oz.*

4 tablespoons good quality white wine,
   such as Chardonnay
6 tablespoons tarragon vinegar
25g / 1oz shallots, finely chopped
1 tablespoon chopped fresh tarragon, plus a little
   extra to finish
1 teaspoon fresh chervil, plus a little extra to
   finish
3 egg yolks, lightly beaten
200ml / 7fl oz clarified butter, melted
cayenne pepper
salt and coarsely milled black pepper

Put the wine, vinegar, shallots, tarragon, chervil and salt and pepper in a saucepan over a high heat and boil until the liquid is reduced by two-thirds. Remove the pan from the heat and allow the reduction to cool slightly.

Put the reduction in the top of a double boiler over gently simmering water, or in a heatproof bowl that will fit over a pan with plenty of room underneath. Put warm water into the pan, then place the basin in the pan, making sure the bottom does not touch the water. Whisk in the egg yolks and continue whisking for about 12 minutes until the sauce is thick and creamy. Remove the sauce from the heat and slowly whisk in the clarified butter. Pass the sauce through a fine non-metallic sieve. Add a little more finely chopped fresh tarragon and chervil and season with a dash of cayenne. Taste and adjust the seasoning, if necessary.

VARIATIONS

Bridge Sauce Stir 2 tablespoons finely diced cooked beetroot and 1 tablespoon finely chopped fresh basil into the completed sauce. Serve with chicken that has been grilled with lots of garlic.

Sauce Choron Lightly sauté 2 tablespoons finely diced seeded and skinned tomatoes in 25g / 1oz butter until just softened, then strain off the excess moisture. Add to the sauce when it is completed. Serve with fish, meat and poultry.

Sauce Fayot Add 2 tablespoons melted meat glaze or beef marrow to the finished sauce. Serve with grilled lamb or chicken.

Sauce Paloise Replace the fresh tarragon in the reduction and finish the sauce with chopped fresh mint and replace the tarragon vinegar with white wine vinegar. Serve with lamb.

Mayonnaise

It is claimed by some that mayonnaise was invented in 1756 by the Duc de Richelieu's chef, while the French under his command were attacking the English at Port Mahon in Minorca. In yet another French fairy tale, it is named after a yolk of egg *(moyeu)* . . .

The egg yolks for this should be at room temperature. There are numerous opinions about which flavourings are best in this, and I prefer to use Dijon mustard for my recipe rather than English, which I find far too strong.

If the mayonnaise curdles, lightly beat 1 egg yolk in a bowl, then quickly whisk in the separated mayonnaise, 1 tablespoon at a time at first, gradually increasing the amount you add until it is all incorporated. *Makes about 450g / 1lb.*

2 egg yolks
little Dijon mustard
3 tablespoons lemon juice
good pinch of salt and freshly milled black pepper
300ml / 10fl oz olive oil
3 tablespoons wine vinegar

Put the egg yolks, mustard, lemon juice and salt and pepper into a large clean bowl. Use a whisk or an electric mixer and beat together well. (You can also make this in a blender.)

Add the olive oil a drop at a time, whisking constantly until the mayonnaise starts to thicken. Add the vinegar and the remaining olive oil more quickly. Taste and adjust the seasoning. Cover and chill until ready to serve. Adding 1 teaspoon boiling water will help to lighten the mayonnaise if it seems too thick.

VARIATIONS

Aïoli Use the same ingredients and method but add 6 crushed garlic cloves to the egg yolks and omit the mustard. Serve with a selection of crisp raw vegetables.

Beetroot Mayonnaise Dissolve one leaf of aspic or gelatine in 2 tablespoons cold water, then add it to the mayonnaise with 4 tablespoons beetroot purée.

Chaudfroid Sauce Dissolve 1 tablespoon powdered gelatine or 2 leaves of gelatine in 2 tablespoons cold water, then whisk the gelatine into the mayonnaise. Cover and chill for at least 5 minutes, then use to coat hard-boiled eggs or decorate hors d'oeuvres. I find this especially useful when I am preparing dishes for a cold buffet.

Coronation Chicken Sauce For each 150g/5oz mayonnaise, beat in 1 tablespoon curry paste, 3 tablespoons thick double cream and freshly milled black pepper to taste. For a chicken salad fit for a queen, fold in chunks of cooked chicken breasts and add a little diced apple, chopped walnuts or sultanas for extra flavour.

Sauce Louis For each 150g/5oz mayonnaise, beat in 3 tablespoons chilli sauce, 2 tablespoons dry sherry, ½ teaspoon Worcestershire sauce, a little grated fresh horseradish and salt and freshly milled black pepper. Serve with a selection of cooked shellfish to make a first-rate seafood cocktail.

Mustard Mayonnaise Use the ingredients and method as for making mayonnaise, but increase the amount of mustard to 150g/5oz. Serve with chicken.

Sauce Rémoulade To 150g/5oz mayonnaise, add 1 tablespoon Dijon mustard and 1 teaspoon each finely chopped capers, gherkins, fresh tarragon and 1 anchovy fillet. Serve with scampi, seafood and chicken.

Russian Sauce For each 150g/5oz mayonnaise, stir in 3 tablespoons lobster sauce (pages 53–4), 1 tablespoon caviar, 1 teaspoon Dijon mustard, 1 teaspoon finely chopped fresh parsley and salt and freshly milled black pepper. Cover and chill for at least 6 hours, then serve with poached fresh lobster meat to make a delicious lobster salad.

Avocado Mystique

This really is a party piece . . . it looks like a bunch of cherries on a plate but it is actually small balls of avocado, melon and mango coated with red mayonnaise. *Serves 4*

red food colouring (optional)
1 quantity beetroot mayonnaise (above)
2 avocados
1 melon
2 mangoes
36 cherries, stalks removed but reserved

If you wish, add a few drops of red food colouring to the beetroot mayonnaise to give it a more pronounced red colour, then set aside.

Use a ball scoop the size of a cherry to scoop out 12 balls of avocado, 12 balls of melon and 12 balls of mango; do not cut the avocado until you are ready to use it.

Use a cocktail stick to dip each of the fruit balls into the beetroot mayonnaise, making sure they are evenly coated.

Carefully arrange the fruit balls on a plain white plate to look like a bunch of cherries. Place the reserved cherry stalks in the holes made by the cocktail sticks.

Demi-glace Sauces

In all the large and prestigious kitchens round the world, chefs make large vats of demi-glace sauce on a regular basis. Professional kitchens are never without a supply, and this is such an important sauce for anyone who takes their cooking seriously that I always have some at hand in the fridge. This is the base for all dark sauces, and it is used in most sauces to be served with meat, poultry and game.

Demi-glace Sauce

Demi-glace sauce is characterized by its smooth texture and dark, glossy finish, so it is important to skim the surface before you strain it. *Makes about 1 litre/1¼ pints.*

> 1 litre/1¾ pints Espagnole sauce (pages 38–9)
> 1 litre/1¾ pints meat stock (pages 20–21)
> salt and freshly milled black pepper

Put the Espagnole sauce and meat stock in a large heavy-bottomed saucepan and simmer until it is reduced by half. Skim the surface well, then pass the sauce through a fine non-metallic sieve. Taste and adjust the seasoning. The sauce is now ready to use, or it can be left to cool and then refrigerated for up to 5 days. Demi-glace sauce can also be frozen for up to 2 months.

VARIATIONS

Madeira Sauce Combine 300ml/10fl oz demi-glace sauce with 3 tablespoons Madeira wine, then taste and adjust the seasoning. Whisk in 25g/1oz unsalted butter and adjust the seasoning again. Serve with steaks.

Rich Madeira Sauce Boil 9 tablespoons Madeira wine, 4 chopped shallots, 2 tablespoons red wine vinegar, 5 black peppercorns and 50ml/2fl oz veal stock (page 21) until reduced by half. Add this to 300ml/10fl oz demi-glace sauce.

Red Wine Demi-glace Sauce Boil 9 tablespoons red wine, 4 chopped shallots, 2 tablespoons red wine vinegar, 5 black peppercorns and 50ml/2fl oz veal stock (page 21) until reduced by half. Add this to 300ml/10fl oz demi-glace sauce.

Bordelaise Sauce

Diced poached beef marrow is the classic ingredient in this sauce, often served with grilled meats. (For a different version of this sauce, made with Espagnole sauce, see pages 38–9.)

For a simple meal, grill sirloin steak or lamb cutlets and fry some sliced onions, wild mushrooms and red, green and yellow peppers cut into julienne strips. Arrange the vegetables on a serving plate, place the meat on top and spoon over a little of this sauce. *Makes about 300ml/10fl oz.*

> 150ml/5fl oz good-quality claret
> 2 tablespoons red wine vinegar
> 50g/2oz shallots or onions, finely chopped
> 1 bay leaf
> 1 sprig of fresh thyme
> pinch of coarsely milled black peppercorns
> 300ml/10fl oz demi-glace sauce (above)
> 75g/3oz beef marrow, diced
> salt and freshly milled black pepper

Place all the ingredients, except the demi-glace sauce and the marrow, into a small saucepan over a high heat and boil until the liquids reduce by at least one-quarter.

Add the demi-glace sauce, lower the heat and simmer for at least 20 minutes. Taste and adjust the seasoning, then pass the sauce through a fine non-metallic sieve. Stir in the beef marrow.

Hunters' Sauce

This sauce, called *sauce chasseur* in French, is usually served with chicken, beef or lamb, but I suggest you try it as a base for vegetable lasagne or a vegetable bake. For a fuller flavour, use red wine or port instead of white wine. *Makes about 600ml/1 pint.*

25g/1oz butter or margarine
25g/1oz shallots or onions, chopped
1 small garlic clove, crushed
50g/2oz button mushrooms, sliced
4 tablespoons dry white wine
4 tablespoons white wine vinegar
100g/4oz tomatoes, skinned and chopped
300ml/10fl oz demi-glace sauce (page 35)
pinch each of finely chopped fresh parsley and
  fresh tarragon
salt and freshly milled black pepper

Melt the butter or margarine in a small saucepan over a medium heat, then add the shallots or onions and fry gently for 2 minutes, stirring frequently. Add the garlic and mushrooms and continue cooking for a further 2 minutes.

Strain off any fat, then add the wine and vinegar. Bring to the boil and continue boiling until the liquids reduce by half.

Add the tomatoes and demi-glace sauce and simmer for 8 minutes. Add the parsley and tarragon, then taste and adjust the seasoning.

Quick Chicken, Hunters' Style

Place 3 thinly sliced chicken breasts into a small casserole with 8 whole shallots and 100g/4oz sliced button mushrooms. Pour over 300ml/10fl oz hunters' sauce and bake at 200°C/400°F/gas mark 6 for 35 minutes until the chicken slices are cooked through and tender.

Devilled Sauce

I have used several versions of this hot, piquant sauce in my career, but I always prefer this recipe, which I have developed. I use rose petal vinegar, instead of the more traditional white wine and vinegar, to make a lighter and more palatable sauce, which can then be served with fresh salmon or lobster. Escoffier's version of *sauce diable*, as this sauce is called in France, includes mangoes, dates, raisins, tomatoes, sugar and vinegar, and tastes very much like a chutney! His sauce is also known as *sauce Escoffier*. *Makes about 250ml / 9fl oz.*

50g / 2oz shallots, chopped
1 teaspoon crushed black peppercorns
2 tablespoons rose petal vinegar (page 16) mixed with a pinch of cayenne pepper,
or
1 tablespoon white wine and 1 tablespoon white wine vinegar mixed together
300ml / 10fl oz demi-glace sauce (page 35)
extra cayenne pepper
salt and freshly milled black pepper

Put the shallots, peppercorns and vinegar with cayenne pepper or wine and vinegar in a saucepan and bring until the liquid is reduced by half.

Add the demi-glace sauce and simmer for 7 minutes. Add cayenne pepper to taste if you have not used the cayenne-flavoured rose petal vinegar, then taste again and adjust the seasoning. You can serve the sauce as it is, or strain it.

Pepper Sauce

The basis for this sauce, commonly known as venison sauce, or *sauce poivrade* as it is called in France, is a good white wine vinegar and shallots. Dr William Kitchiner quotes from *La Cuisinière Bourgeoise* (1827) in a second edition of *The Cook's Oracle*:

> Put a bit of butter as big as an egg into a stewpan with two or three (bits of) onion, carrot, and turnip, cut into slices, two shallots, two cloves, a bay leaf, thyme, and basil, keep turning them in the pan till they get a little colour, – shake in some flour, and add a glass of red Wine, a glass of water, and a spoonful of Vinegar, and a little Pepper and Salt, boil half an hour, skim and strain it.

Several chefs that I know use my vinegar method for this sauce. It is also included in the City and Guilds course book, but, unfortunately, with a few changes I cannot endorse, such as the use of crushed peppercorns rather than whole one and a mixture of white wine and vinegar rather than all vinegar. That version also includes celery, which I think should be completely forbidden. This, however, is the recipe I approve of. *Makes about 300ml / 10fl oz.*

4 tablespoons tarragon vinegar
6 black peppercorns
300ml / 10fl oz demi-glace sauce (page 35)
salt and freshly milled black pepper

for the mirepoix
25g / 1oz butter
50g / 2oz carrot, finely diced
50g / 2oz shallots, finely diced
1 sprig of fresh parsley
1 bay leaf
a little fresh thyme

Melt the butter for the mirepoix in a medium saucepan over a very low heat, then add the remaining mirepoix ingredients and cook until they are brown. Strain the vegetables to remove the fat, then return them to the pan.

Add the tarragon vinegar and peppercorns and boil until the vinegar is reduced by half. Add the demi-glace sauce and simmer for 25 minutes. Taste and adjust the seasoning.

VARIATION

Sauce Diane Add 150ml/5fl oz whipped cream, 1 truffle cut into julienne strips and 1 finely chopped hard-boiled egg. Serve this hot with steaks and veal.

Sauce Piquante

This is used for left-over meats, and is excellent for serving on cold buffets or when you have unexpected guests and want to make a good impression with very little time. The French serve this sauce with veal tongue. I prefer it, however, with slices of York ham layered with silverside of beef. You can put a little extra life into this sauce by adding a stronger red wine demi-glace sauce (page 35) made with a sweet shallot vinegar and some Dijon mustard. *Makes about 225ml/8fl oz.*

25g/1oz butter
50g/2oz onion, finely chopped
2 tablespoons tarragon vinegar
300ml/10fl oz demi-glace sauce (page 35)
1 tablespoon tomato purée
50g/2oz gherkins, finely chopped
1 teaspoon chopped fresh parsley
1 teaspoon each of chopped fresh tarragon and
  chervil
salt and freshly milled black pepper

Melt the butter in a saucepan over a medium heat, add the onion and cook until it is lightly browned, stirring frequently. Add the vinegar and continue cooking until it is reduced to almost nothing.

Add the demi-glace sauce and tomato purée and simmer for 10 minutes. Add the gherkins and parsley, tarragon and chervil. Taste and adjust the seasoning.

Espagnole Sauce

Without doubt, this is one of the great French classics. This basic sauce, also called brown sauce in English, is very important to English and French chefs, as it is the foundation for so many other sauces. It is to this end that the great chefs of England and France agree that there are no shortcuts to making this – it should take at least 4½ hours to make – and not a single error can be permitted.

My addition of vinegar in this recipe, however, is not a new idea. I have an 1888 recipe that suggests including a 'glass' of vinegar or sherry, and Dr William Kitchiner also suggests in 1817, in *The Cook's Oracle*, that tarragon vinegar makes a good variation. *Makes about 500ml/¾ pint.*

100g/4oz brown roux (page 23)
25g/1oz tomato purée
1 litre/1¾ pints meat stock (pages 20–21), boiling
2 tablespoons wine vinegar
salt and freshly milled black pepper

for the mirepoix
2 tablespoons cooking oil or 25g/1oz butter
100g/4oz raw back bacon, finely diced
100g/4oz carrot, finely diced
100g/4oz onion, finely diced
50g/2oz celery, finely diced

50g/2oz leeks, finely diced
50g/2oz fresh fennel, finely diced
1 sprig of fresh thyme
1 small bay leaf

Put the roux and tomato purée in a large saucepan over a low heat, then slowly stir in the meat stock and vinegar and simmer for about 10 minutes.

In a separate saucepan, heat the oil or melt the butter and cook all the mirepoix ingredients for about 4 minutes until the vegetable are a soft golden colour, stirring frequently.

Strain the vegetables and herbs to remove the excess fat, then add them to the sauce. Bring to the boil, then cover, lower the heat and simmer for at least 4 hours. Taste and adjust the seasoning. Pass through a fine non-metallic sieve into a clean saucepan. The sauce is now ready to use, or it can be stored in a covered container in the refrigerator for up to 5 days. Brown sauce also freezes for up to 2 months.

VARIATION

Pepper Sauce For a simple sauce to serve with steak au poivre, add 1 tablespoon green peppercorns, extra freshly ground black pepper and 2 tablespoons double cream to 150ml/5fl oz brown sauce.

Sauce Bigarade

A popular French sauce for game and duck. It is very important that only a Seville orange is used in this recipe because of its sharp flavour. *Makes about 250ml/9fl oz.*

finely julienned rind and juice of 1 Seville orange
juice of 1 lemon
225ml/8fl oz Espagnole sauce (pages 38–9)
4 tablespoons good-quality red wine, such as
   Burgundy
1 tablespoon redcurrant jelly
pinch of cayenne pepper
salt

Put the orange rind and a little water into a saucepan and bring to the boil, then lower the heat and simmer until the rind is tender.

Drain the rind and return it to the pan with the orange juice, lemon juice, Espagnole sauce, wine, redcurrant jelly, cayenne and salt to taste. Bring the sauce to the boil, then lower the heat and simmer for 5 minutes.

Wine Sauces

Marchand de vin is the French term for a wine merchant, and it is often used in French recipe titles to denote that a sauce is made with wine. Perhaps the best known of these sauce are *sauce bordelaise* and *sauce bourguignonne*, yet as I look through my large cookery book collection, I find many variations and little agreement on exactly what wines these sauces should be made with.

French chef Raymond Oliver, for example, specified half a bottle of red wine in his *sauce bordelaise* recipe, while Auguste Escoffier's recipe called for one bottle of good red wine. André L. Simon stated in his *Guide to Good Foods and Wine* (1949) that *sauce bourguignonne* should be more highly seasoned than *sauce bordelaise* and made with red Burgundy in place of Claret. I've include a recipe on page 35 for Bordelaise sauce that is made with demi-glace sauce, rather than the Espagnole sauce in the recipe below. This just goes to illustrate how much confusion exists.

Charles Elmé Francatelli, who was Queen Victoria's head chef, provided the following recipe for *sauce bourguignotte* in his *Cook's Guide* (1869): 'Put into a small stewpan twenty-four fried button onions, twelve mushrooms, twelve small truffles; add a glass of red wine and a half pint of brown sauce (demi-glace); boil together for five minutes and serve.'

Bordelaise Sauce

This recipe includes red Medoc, one of the traditional red wines of the Bordeaux region, but I have also found recipes for this sauce made with white wine in several of my old cookery books. (See page 35 for a different version.) Serve this red-wine version with game or steaks. *Makes about 200ml / 7fl oz.*

50g / 2oz butter
6 shallots, finely chopped
½ garlic clove, crushed
½ bottle of red Medoc wine
50g / 2oz beef marrow, warm
150ml / 5fl oz Espagnole sauce (pages 38–9)
1 teaspoon chopped fresh parsley
salt and freshly milled black pepper

Melt the butter in a saucepan over a medium heat, add the shallots and garlic and lightly fry, stirring frequently. Stir in the wine and boil until it reduced by one-third.

Add the beef marrow and Espagnole sauce and season with salt and pepper. Simmer for a further 6 minutes, then add the parsley and serve.

VARIATIONS

Sauce Bourguignonne Use the same ingredients and method as for Bordelaise sauce, but add 20 sautéed button mushrooms and replace the Medoc wine with a rich red Burgundy.

Sauce Moelle Use the same ingredients and method as for Bordelaise sauce, but use a dry white wine, instead of red.

Traditional English Sauces

Some Famous English Sauces

Prince Francesco Caraccioli, a late 18th-century Italian admiral, is reputed to have said that in England there were sixty religions but only one sauce. Yet, it is difficult to imagine which sauce he had in mind, as English cookery books of his period contained a wide variety, from *sauce Robart*, to verjuice and a succulent zest sauce.

My co-author Colin Cooper-English and I spent eight years researching *Dr William Kitchiner, A Regency Eccentric*, a study of the author of *The Cook's Oracle*, written in 1817. The splendid Kitchiner created so many unique sauces that he should have been recognized as the king of sauces, and much of his work dates from Caraccioli's time. Some of his creations are now out of fashion, such as his lemon and liver sauce, while others have become 'typical' English sauces that still enjoy popularity, such as gooseberry sauce served with mackerel. I have included many of these old recipes, in their original form, for your interest and enjoyment.

Kitchiner's *The Cook's Oracle* was sophisticated enough to include sauces of undoubted Continental origin, including the famous and familiar béchamel sauce. Although this is not an English sauce, it is believed to be the one Caraccioli had in mind when he uttered his famous epigram. His was perhaps an understandable error, as béchamel is one of the foundation sauces that provides the base for so many other sauces. It exists not only in its own right as a fairly simple white sauce, but it can be transformed into other sauces with the addition of other ingredients, such as anchovy essence, shrimps, parsley and capers, to list just a few.

Harvey's Sauce

The name of Harvey's sauce, another popular English sauce of the period, is derived from a Bedfont innkeeper who popularized the sauce, but had absolutely nothing to do with its invention.

I have come across four versions of the origins of Harvey's sauce, originally known as Mrs Combers' Sauce, and this is the one I favour.

Captain Charles Combers (born 1752) was a member of the Quorn Hunt. Once on his way to Leicester, in 1780, he made his customary stop at the Black Dog Inn, Bedfont, which was then kept by a man named Peter Harvey. Combers ordered a steak and sent his servant to fetch from his carriage a bottle which contained this admirable sauce: a mixture of walnut ketchup, mushroom ketchup, soy sauce, garlic, sprats and cayenne pepper. Combers poured some on his plate, stirred it into the steak's gravy, and then asked Harvey to taste the mixture. The host pronounced it to be 'a most excellent relish'.

According to the legend, Combers said: 'Well, Mr Harvey, I shall leave the bottle with you to use till my return. Only be careful to reserve enough for me.' On the following day Harvey had to provide a wedding dinner and cater for several smaller parties. He introduced the sauce, and it was afforded such general satisfaction that the contents of the bottle were soon exhausted.

When Captain Combers returned, a shame-faced Harvey had to confess that none of the sauce remained. Combers received the news in generous spirit. 'Never mind,' he said, according to the legend. 'I can make some more from my mother's recipe. And by the way I will give you a copy of it.'

Charles Combers carried out his promise, and Harvey soon began to make the sauce for use on the tables in his inn. Before long it was made in larger and larger quantities for the guests to take away, and he sent it to shops in London, advertising it as Harvey's sauce. Its popularity continued to grow and its sales realized a large income. Harvey sold the recipe to Elizabeth Lazenby & Son in 1780 for an annuity of £500 a year.

Almost one hundred years later, in 1870, this sauce was the subject of legal action. The Rolls Court ruled that there was no copyright on the recipe, and anyone could make or sell it, providing they did not bottle it in a manner that imitated any other firm's label in a recognizable form.

I think it is interesting to note that Charles Elmé Francatelli, Queen Victoria's head chef, mixed Harvey's sauce, anchovies, redcurrant jelly and pepper sauce with a glass of port to create his reform sauce, a recipe he made for the queen when he was head of the royal kitchens. (See page 55 for his recipe.)

Harvey, whose Inn commands a view
Of Bedfont's Church and churchyard too,
Where yew-trees into peacocks shorn
In vegetables torture mourn.

The Rudiments of Cookery, from *The Cook's Oracle* (1817)

The Spirit of each dish, and Zest of all,
Is what ingenious Cooks the Relish call;
For though the market sends in loads of
    food,
They all are tasteless, till that makes them
    good.

King's Art of Cookery.

The most homely fare may be made relishing, and the most excellent and independent, improved by a well made Sauce; – as the most perfect Picture may, by being well varnished.

We have, therefore, endeavoured to give the plainest directions, how to produce, with the least trouble and expense possible – all the various compositions the English kitchen affords for the amusement of honest JOHN BULL, – and hope to present such a wholesome and palatable variety as will suit all tastes and pockets, so that a Cook may give satisfaction in all families: the more combinations of this sort she is acquainted with, the better she will comprehend the management of every one of them.

We have rejected some Outlandish Farragoes, from a conviction they were by no means adapted to an English palate, if they have been received into some English books, for the sake of swelling the volume, we believe they will never be received by an Englishman's stomach, unless for the reason they were admitted into the Cookery book; i.e. because he has nothing else to put into it.

Let your Sauces each display a decided character; send up your PLAIN SAUCES (Oyster, Lobster, &c.) as pure as possible;– they should taste of the materials from which they take their name.

The imagination of most Cooks, is so incessantly on the hunt for a Relish, – that they seem to think they cannot make sauce sufficiently savoury, without putting into it everything that was ever eaten;– and supposing every addition must be an improvement, they frequently over power the natural flavour of their PLAIN SAUCES, by over loading them with salt and spices, &c.:– but remember, these will be deteriorated by any addition, save only just salt enough to awaken the Palate.

Why have Clove and Allspice, – or Mace and Nutmeg in the same sauce, – or Marjoram, Thyme, and Savoury : – or Onions and Leeks, Eshallots and Garlick:– one will very well supply the place of the other, and the frugal Cook may save something considerable by attending to this, to the advantage of her employers, and her own time and trouble.

You might as well, to make Soup, order one quart of water from the Thames, another from the New River, a third from Hampstead, and a fourth from Chelsea, with a certain portion of Spring and Rain Water.

Seventeenth-century Sauces

I've taken the following recipes from the 1933 edition of *Good Things in England* by Florence White.

Oyster Sauce for Roast Shoulder of Mutton
Oysters with roast or boiled mutton, or made into a pudding, pie or hot-pot with mutton, are a distinctive feature of cookery in England, dating from the days of the Romans.

Gravy, white wine, oyster liquor in which oysters have been parboiled, a few oysters, thicken with yolk of egg (the shoulder may be stuffed with oysters cut into bits, seasoned with pepper, salt, a little anchovy chopped fine, a few breadcrumbs, mingled with the yolk of one or two raw eggs and a little ham cut small). Garnish with slic't lemon.

Sauce for Roast Shoulder of Mutton without Oysters

Gravy, claret, pepper, grated nutmeg; slic't lemon and broom buds. Garnish the mutton with barberries and slic't lemon.

The following two recipes illustrate that sauces to serve with pork haven't changed much in the past 300 years:

Gravy, chopped sage and onions boiled together with some pepper.
Apples pared, quartered and boiled in fair water, with some sugar and butter.

Finally, here are three traditional recipes for game.

Pigeon Sauce
Gravy and juice of orange, or gravy, claret wine and an onion stewed together with a little salt.

Sauce for Any Land Fowl, Game or Turkey etc
Stamp small nuts to a paste, with bread, nutmeg, pepper, saffron, cloves, juice or orange, and strong broth, boil them together pretty thick and strain.

Sauce for Pork, Goslings, Chicken, Lamb or Kid
Juice of green wheat (frumenty), lemon, bread and sugar.

Worcestershire Sauce

What is Lord Sandys' Sauce? Nothing less than the best known sauce in the world, and perhaps nowadays it would be regarded as England's 'one sauce', the famous Worcestershire sauce. Lea & Perrins are the original makers, but today other firms make this thin, dark brown condiment as well.

Whoever makes it, however, it is known as 'Worcestershire sauce' and it has been so known for more than 150 years.

Worcestershire sauce evolved – probably with a few years of trial and error by Indian cooks in Bengal – and was brought to England in 1805 by Baron Sandys of Ombersly Court, in Worcestershire, when he retired from the governorship of Bengal. In January 1825, William Perrins and John Wheeley Lea, Worcester chemists, experimented in making the sauce and founded a company to produce it on a commercial scale. By 1838 they had agents all over the world, and, eventually, both partners retired multi-millionaires.

Gravy and Brown Sauce

Some of the best English recipes – roast beef, shepherd's pie and steak and kidney pie, for example – have their origins linked with a good basic gravy. As my good friend Francis Coulson, chef/proprietor of Sharrow Bay Hotel on Ullswater in Cumbria, observed in his television programme *Reflections of Sharrow*: 'Let's us not decry the word gravy. It is part of our heritage.'

From *The Cook & Householder's Dictionary* (1823) by Mrs Mary Eaton:

Sauce for Wild Fowl: Simmer a tea-cupful of port wine, the same good quantity of good meat gravy , a little shalot, a little pepper and salt, a grate of nutmeg, and a bit of mace, for ten minutes. Put a piece of butter, and flour; give it all one boil, and pour it through the birds.

Perfect Gravy

When I want to serve onion gravy with Yorkshire puddings, I just add the juice from the roast beef to this recipe with an extra finely chopped onion. This recipe is dedicated to Francis Coulson. *Makes about 600ml/1 pint.*

50g/2oz beef dripping
1 onion, finely diced
1 carrot, finely diced
2 rashers best back bacon, rind and any gristle removed and finely chopped
2 tablespoons dry sherry
2 tablespoons red wine vinegar
50g/2oz plain flour
600ml/1 pint meat stock (pages 20–21)
1 bouquet garni
1 tablespoon tomato purée
salt and freshly milled black pepper

Melt the dripping in a heavy based saucepan over a medium heat. Add the onion, carrot and bacon and fry for 10 minutes until light brown, stirring frequently. Add the sherry and vinegar and continue cooking for 3 minutes.

Blend in the flour, stirring the roux for 10–12 minutes until it is brown. Gradually add half the beef stock, stirring constantly until the mixture has cooked through and thickened. Bring to the boil and add the bouquet garni, then lower the heat and simmer, uncovered, for 30 minutes. Stir in the tomato purée, remaining beef stock and salt and pepper, then continue simmering and skimming the surface as necessary for a further 30 minutes. Taste and adjust the seasoning all the time.

Strain through a fine non-metallic sieve, skim off any extra fat and serve.

VARIATION

Tomato Sauce Just add an extra 100g/4oz tomato purée to the perfect gravy recipe to make a light tomato sauce. Serve with chicken, veal and steaks.

'A Good Gravy Soop'

I could not resist including this recipe from *The Art of Cookery, Made Plain and Easy, By a Lady* (1747). I think it provides a good insight into how much hard work was involved in the preparation of food during the 18th century. It also gives the reader a glimpse into the type of produce readily available in 1747, such as truffles and morels, which can be very difficult to purchase today . . . and which are expensive.

I also think it is interesting to note that the cost of making this gravy in 1747 was just one shilling, which would have kept a family of four for one month. In 1995, however, I have estimated it would cost about £40.

I've reproduced the recipe as it is written, with the letter *f* used to indicate the letter *s*.

TAKE a Pound of Beef, a Pound of Veal, and a Pound of Mutton, cut and hacked to Pieces, put it into two Gallons of Water, with an Old Cock, beat to Pieces, a piece of Carrot, the Upper Cruft of a Penny-loaf toafted very crifp, a little bundle of Sweet Herbs, an Onion, a tea Spoonful of black Pepper, and one of white Pepper, four or five Blades of Mace, and four Cloves. Cover it, and let it ftew over a flow Fire, till half is wafted, then ftrain it off, and put it into a Clean Sauce-pan, with two or three large Spoonfuls of Rafpings clean fifted, half an Ounce of Truffles and Morels, three or four Heads of Salary wafhed very clean, and cut fmall an Ox's Palate, firft boiled tender, and cut into Pieces, a few Cock's Combs, a few of the little Hearts of young Savoys, cover it clofe, and let it fimmer very foftly over a flow Fire for two Hours; then have ready a French Role fry'd, and a few Forced-meat Balls fry'd, put them into your Difh, and pour in your Soop. You may boil a Leg of Veal, and a leg of Beef, and as many fine things as you pleafe; but I believe you will find this rich and high enough.

Brown Onion Sauce

I have a great love for liver, bacon and onions, and I think this is the ideal sauce to serve with them. The French call this *sauce lyonnaise*. *Makes about 300ml/10fl oz.*

25g/1oz unsalted butter
225g/8oz onions, sliced
2 tablespoons red wine vinegar
1 tablespoon port
300ml/10fl oz demi-glace sauce (page 35)

Melt the butter in a large saucepan over a medium heat, then add the onions, cover and fry gently for 4 minutes until they are transparent.

Add the port and red wine vinegar and cook until the liquid is completely absorbed.

Add the demi-glace sauce and simmer for 6 minutes. Taste and adjust the seasoning.

Liver, Bacon and Onions with Brown Onion Sauce

Preheat the oven to 200°C/400°F/gas mark 6. Thinly slice 450g/1lb lambs' liver, cut 225g/8oz rindless back bacon into thin strips and very thinly slice 225g/8oz onions.

Melt 2 tablespoons cooking oil in a flame-proof casserole over a medium heat. Lightly fry the liver, bacon and onions together for 4 minutes. Pour in 50ml/2fl oz brown onion sauce and bake for 20 minutes. Serve with parsley croûtons. *Serves 4.*

Game Sauces

Many people think only of a traditional Cumberland sauce when they are asked to name a game sauce, yet there are two categories of these sauces. The first, which includes Cumberland sauce, is for serving with small game, such as hare, quail, partridge, pheasant, wild duck and so on. The second category includes pepper sauce and is intended for serving with larger game, such as wild boar.

In 1783 John Farley wrote *The London Art Of Cookery*, which included this recipe for venison sauce: 'currant jelly warmed; or half pint of red wine, with a quarter of a pound of sugar, simmered over a clear fire for five or six minutes; or half a pint of vinegar, and a quarter pound of sugar, simmered till it be a syrup.'

Old English Game Sauce

For this modern game sauce, I have borrowed from the genius of Charles Elmé Francatelli's venison sauce, which he made for Queen Victoria when he was her personal chef. *Makes about 225ml/8fl oz.*

2 tablespoons orange and green peppercorn
    vinegar (page 15)
200g/7oz redcurrant jelly
2 tablespoons port
1 blade of mace
1 small stick of cinnamon
1 bay leaf
1 tablespoon chopped lemon rind
2 shallots, finely chopped
pinch of salt
25g/1oz mushrooms, coarsely chopped
1 tablespoon capers, finely chopped
4 black and 4 white peppercorns, freshly milled

Put the orange and green pepper vinegar, redcurrant jelly, port, mace, cinnamon, bay leaf, lemon rind and finely chopped shallots into a saucepan over a high heat and bring to the boil. Reduce the heat and simmer for 12 minutes, then add the salt.

Pass the sauce through a fine non-metallic sieve into a sauce boat. Sprinkle with the mushrooms, capers and freshly milled peppercorns, blending them into the sauce before serving.

Cumberland Sauce

I have several 18th- and 19th-century cookery books that do not agree about the ingredients for Cumberland sauce. I would like to think that this English version is the true recipe. *Makes about 225g/8oz.*

1 small onion, finely chopped
3 tablespoons red wine vinegar
finely shredded rind and juice of 1 orange
finely shredded rind and juice of 1 lemon
6 tablespoons redcurrant jelly
6 tablespoons port
½ teaspoon prepared English mustard
  pinch of cayenne pepper
1 teaspoon sugar

Put the onion and wine vinegar in a saucepan and simmer for 2 minutes. Add the orange and lemon rinds with a little of the juices and continue simmering for a further 2 minutes. Put the sauce into a clear bowl and allow it to cool. Stir in the remaining juices, redcurrant jelly, port, mustard, cayenne pepper and sugar and mix together thoroughly. Add the rest of the ingredients and mix thoroughly. The sauce is ready to use.

Rosa's Quail Pudding

One of my ambitions in life is to research and write every recipe belonging to Rosa Lewis, whose life story was the inspiration for the classic television series, *The Duchess of Duke Street*. Much of the script was based on her time as chef/proprietor of the Cavendish Hotel, on London's Jermyn Street. She was famous for her game sauces and her quail pudding, created for her long-time friend Edward VII. Rosa also made her quail pudding for White's, one of London's oldest gentlemen's clubs, and she was advised by Auguste Escoffier, one of her regular clients.

If you don't want to spend the time steaming the pudding, serve the quail meat sliced with vegetables and the sauce in a sauce boat. If you don't like quail, you can also make this recipe with a chicken breast and substituting chicken stock (page 21) for the game stock. I include this recipe for Julian Groom and everyone at the Cavendish Hotel. *Serves 2.*

50g/2oz herb butter (page 30)
8 quail breasts, skin removed
75g/3oz button mushrooms
50g/2oz shallots, sliced
150ml/5fl oz fresh orange juice
1 sprig of fresh thyme
4 tablespoons brandy
salt and freshly milled black pepper
150ml/5fl oz game sauce (page 47)
225g/8oz my grandmother's suet pastry (below)

Melt the herb butter in a large frying pan over a medium heat. Add the quail breasts, button mushrooms and shallots and pan-fry for about 6 minutes. Remove the breasts from the pan.

Add the orange juice, thyme, brandy and seasoning to the pan and simmer for at least 20 minutes until the liquid is reduced by half.

Add the game sauce and simmer to reduce by half again. Place the quail meat and game sauce into a 20cm/8in pudding basin, lined with the suet pastry. Cover the top of the basin with several layers of foil, then steam the pudding in a covered saucepan for 2 hours, topping up the pan with extra water as necessary.

My Grandmother's Suet Pastry

Place 225g/8oz self-rising flour, 75g/3oz softened butter and 50g/2oz fresh or shredded suet in a bowl and rub together with your fingertips until the mixture resembles fine breadcrumbs. Mix 1 egg (size 3) and 1 tablespoon water together.

Make a well in the centre of the flour and suet mixture and pour in the egg. Mix together until a soft paste forms. Turn out on to a floured work surface and knead into a soft dough. Roll out and use half to line the pudding basin and freeze the remainder until required. *Makes about 450g/1lb.*

From *Warnes Model Cookery* (1868) by Mary Jewry:

SAUCE FOR HARE: One carrot; one onion; one clove; one blade of mace; two ounces of butter; a wineglass of vinegar; twelve tablespoons of brown sauce; three of broth; a little horseradish two tablespoonfuls of currant jelly. Cut a carrot and an onion into slices, put them into a stewpan with a blade of mace, a clove, one bunch of thyme, and two ounces of butter, brown them lightly, then stir in the wineglass of vinegar, three tablespoons of broth (Meat stock), the brown sauce (demi-glaze), &c; add the currant jelly, strain the sauce through a sieve, and serve with hare or venison.

A Selection of Traditional English Sauces

Apple Sauce

The great British pork sauce recipe. *Makes about 400g / 14oz.*

15g / ½oz butter
450g / 1lb Bramley apples, peeled, cored and
   chopped
2 tablespoons water
2 tablespoons caster sugar
1 teaspoon tarragon vinegar
pinch of ground cloves
salt and freshly ground black pepper

Melt the butter in a saucepan over a medium heat, then add the apples with the water. Cover and cook gently for 8 minutes.

Remove the pan from the heat and mash the apples to a soft smooth mixture. Stir in the sugar, vinegar and cloves. Re-heat, stirring all the time. Taste and adjust the seasoning.

Bread Sauce

This sauce came into being in medieval times when bread was a staple food so breadcrumbs were plentiful, and flour wasn't yet used as a thickener. It has never gone out of fashion, and is still a regular feature of Christmas feasts. In Elizabeth Raffald's *The Experienced English Housekeeper* this recipe for bread sauce is listed as Sauce for a Turkey:

Cut the crust off a penny-loaf, cut the rest in thin slices, put in cold water, with a few peppercorns, a little salt and onion, boil it till the bread is quite soft, then beat it well, put in a quarter of a pound of butter, two spoonfuls of thick cream, and put into a basin.

I think my 20th-century version of bread sauce is excellent with game, roast chicken and, of course, the traditional roast turkey for Christmas dinner. Bread sauce should never be re-boiled and take care not to over-cook it or it will become a 'gooey' mess. *Makes about 400g / 14oz.*

6 cloves
1 onion, peeled
450ml / 15fl oz milk
pinch of mace
4 black peppercorns
225g / 8oz fresh white breadcrumbs
15g / ½ oz butter
2 tablespoons double cream
salt and freshly milled black pepper

Stick the cloves into the onion, then put the onion into a saucepan with the milk, mace and peppercorns. Bring to the boil, then remove the pan from the heat, cover and leave the milk to infuse for 35 minutes.

Strain the milk through a fine sieve into another clean pan and stir in the breadcrumbs. Return the pan to the heat and stir continuously for 4–6 minutes until the mixture becomes quite thick.

Season the sauce well, then stir in the cream and butter. Taste and adjust the seasoning if necessary. Serve warm.

Chestnut Sauce

In *The Art of Cookery* (1747) Hannah Glasse gives these instructions for chestnut sauce: 'Take some roasted Chestnuts and put them into some good gravy with a little white wine, and thicken it with a piece of butter rolled in flour.'

I serve this modern version with venison steaks and grouse. It also tastes very good with boiled ham. *Makes about 300ml/10fl oz.*

24 chestnuts, slit along one side
25g/1oz butter
8 button mushrooms, finely chopped
300ml/10fl oz meat stock (pages 20–21)
4 tablespoons cranberry juice (optional)
salt and freshly milled black pepper

Place the chestnuts into a large saucepan with a little water and bring to the boil, then lower the heat and simmer for 25 minutes until they are tender.

Drain the chestnuts and remove the shells and skins while they are still hot. Put them into a blender or food processor and process until they form a thick paste, or rub them through a fine sieve.

Place the chestnut mixture into another saucepan with the butter, mushrooms and meat stock and boil for 10 minutes. If I am serving this with game, I add a little cranberry juice at this point. Taste and adjust the seasoning.

Cranberry Sauce

There is disagreement about whether this sauce is British or Scandinavian. I suspect it is a bit of both really, as we serve it in England with roast turkey throughout the festive Christmas season, and the Swedes serve it with reindeer. The Americans have a real love affair with cranberries, and roast turkey with cranberry sauce is virtually a national dish for Thanksgiving, the fourth Thursday in November. American cranberry sauce, however, tends to be a great deal sweeter than either the British or Scandinavian versions. You can also use honey instead of sugar for a more flavourful taste. *Makes about 450g/1lb.*

450g/1lb fresh cranberries
300ml/10fl oz water
100g/4oz brown sugar

Stew the cranberries in the water until they 'pop', then strain them and rub them through a fine sieve into the rinsed-out saucepan.

Stir in the brown sugar until it dissolves, then re-heat the sauce.

Currant Sauce

Here's a 19th-century recipe for a piquant sauce to serve with venison and hare. *Makes about 350g/12oz.*

25g/1oz butter
50g/2oz dried currants
25g/1oz plain flour
300ml/10fl oz chicken stock (page 21)
1 tablespoon brown sugar
150ml/5fl oz sweet white wine
1 tablespoon white wine vinegar
finely grated rind of 1 lemon
4 tablespoons lemon juice
freshly grated nutmeg
pinch of ground cloves
freshly grated root ginger
salt and freshly milled black pepper

Melt the butter in a saucepan over a medium heat, then add the currants and cook for 1 minute, stirring occasionally. Blend in the flour and continue cooking for 4 minutes, stirring frequently.

Pour in the stock and bring to the boil, then lower the heat and simmer for 5 minutes. Add the remaining ingredients and return to the boil, then lower the heat and simmer for a further 20 minutes, stirring all the time. Taste and adjust the seasoning. Pass the sauce through a fine non-metallic sieve, then cover and chill until required. Serve chilled.

VARIATION
Sultana Sauce Use the same ingredients and method as for the currant sauce, but substitute sultanas for the currants. Serve with game.

Curry Sauce

Curries have become very popular throughout the world, and the variety is vast. Malaysian curries, for example, are lighter in texture than those made in India, Pakistan, Burma, Vietnam and Ceylon. Yet, no matter what kind of curry is made, turmeric, ginger, garlic and chilli are always included in the sauce.

Most Indian curries are not, in fact, the hot and fiery things we so often get in England, where the average cook seems to cherish the idea that the hotter the curry the more genuinely Indian it becomes. Curry sauce, as prepared by Indian cooks, has a subtle and pleasing flavour. Indian cookery writer Madhur Jaffrey once told me it is not difficult to master Indian spices, if you don't have a clumsy hand!

The French call this *sauce kari*, and it is the one sauce they have never mastered. I make my sauce using Dr William Kitchiner's wonderful recipe of 1817.

The most important ingredient is a very good curry powder, and I use the recipe below, which was quite openly copied by Isabella Beeton in *The Book of Household Management* (1861) from Dr Kitchiner's recipe. *The sauce recipe makes about 350ml/12fl oz.*

50g/2oz butter
100g/4oz onion, finely sliced
1 garlic clove, crushed
1 tablespoon curry powder (below)
25g/1oz plain flour
175ml/6fl oz coconut milk
1 tablespoon tomato purée
350ml/12fl oz chicken stock (page 21)
25g/1oz peeled and cored apple, chopped
25g/1oz each of sultanas and raisins
natural yogurt or sour cream (optional)
salt and freshly milled black pepper

for the curry powder
75g / 3oz coriander seeds
75g / 3oz turmeric
25g / 1oz each of the following: black peppercorns,
   dry English mustard, peeled fresh ginger,
   allspice berries, cardamom seeds, cayenne
   pepper, cumin seeds, garlic powder and 5 cloves

First make the curry powder by pounding all the ingredients together until they form a fine powder. Store in an air-tight container and use as required.

Melt the butter in a large saucepan, then add the onion and garlic and fry until they are softened. Stir in the curry powder and flour and continue frying gently for 5 minutes, stirring frequently.

Add the coconut milk, tomato purée and the stock, stirring, to make a smooth sauce. Add the apple, sultanas and raisins and seasoning, then simmer for at least 40 minutes, stirring occasionally. Taste and adjust the seasoning. If the flavour is too hot, stir in a little natural yogurt or sour cream; do not let the sauce boil after these are added or they may curdle.

Gooseberry Sauce

This classic sauce dates to the 17th century, and has always been served with mackerel. For a stronger-flavoured sauce, use fish stock (pages 19–20) instead of water when stewing the gooseberries. *Makes about 200g / 7 oz.*

225g / 8oz gooseberries
150ml / 5fl oz water
25g / 1oz butter
25g / 1oz sugar
juice of 1 lemon
freshly grated nutmeg
fresh snipped chives and finely chopped fresh
   sorrel (optional)
salt and freshly milled black pepper

Slowly stew gooseberries very gently with the water and butter until they are pulpy, then beat them with a wire whisk until a smooth sauce forms.

Re-heat the sauce and stir in the sugar, lemon juice and nutmet to taste. Taste and adjust the seasoning. Add a few chives or some sorrel if you desire.

Ham Sauce

An 1845 recipe from *Francatelli's Cook's Guide* by Charles Elmé Francatelli, Queen Victoria's chef. Serve with veal cutlets or any grilled meat. *Makes about 250ml / 9fl oz.*

25g / 1oz butter
50g / 2oz cooked ham, finely shredded
3 shallots, finely chopped
1 teaspoon snipped fresh chives
300ml / 10fl oz Espagnole sauce (pages 38–9)
2 tablespoons lemon juice
1 teaspoon chopped fresh parsley
freshly milled black pepper

Melt the butter in a large saucepan over a medium heat, then add the ham, shallots and chives and cook for 4 minutes, stirring frequently.

Stir in the Espagnole sauce and lemon juice. Taste and adjust the seasoning and stir in the parsley.

Horseradish Sauce or Roast Beef Sauce

Also known as Albert sauce, this is very similar to the French *sauce raifort*, in which the fresh horseradish is soaked in milk with salt and pepper and a little lemon juice and cream stirred in just before serving.

I have used fromage frais instead of the cream, which gives a sharper, less creamy taste, but the sauce is healthier with a lower fat content. *Makes about 175ml/6fl oz.*

150ml/5fl oz double cream
50g/2oz fresh horseradish, peeled and grated
pinch of dry English mustard
2 teaspoons white wine vinegar
1 teaspoon caster sugar
salt and freshly milled black pepper

Very quickly whisk the cream until it is thick, then fold in the horseradish and all the other ingredients one at a time. Cover and chill until ready to serve.

Lobster Sauce

There is only one man I can think of who could create a sauce fit for our Queen and that was my good friend, Silvino Trompetto, MBE, former *maître-chef de cuisine* at the Savoy Hotel in London for several years. Paolo Contarini, a former general manager of the Savoy, paid this tribute to Silvino in *The Savoy was My Oyster*:

He has quite deservedly been called one of the great chefs of the twentieth century. To have a Lobster Newburg – slices of lobster cooked in butter, brandy and Marsala, and served in a cream sauce thickened with coral of the lobster – made by him is an experience that one is unlikely to repeat elsewhere.

This is one of my favourite sauces, and it can be served hot or cold with almost any seafood dish. Using a lobster to make a sauce may seem very extravagant, but it really is the only way to make a sauce of this quality.

I always top this sauce with Tromp's lobster butter and I've included the recipe on page 30. *Makes about 450ml/15fl oz.*

1 kg/2¼ lb hen lobster (really fresh)
75g/3oz best quality butter
100g/4oz shallots, finely chopped
50g/2oz celeriac, finely chopped
100g/4oz carrot, roughly cut
4 tablespoons brandy
2 tablespoons honey and caper vinegar (page 15)
75g/3oz plain flour
100g/4oz tomato purée
1 litre/1¾ pints chicken stock (page 21)
150ml/5fl oz Madeira
150ml/5fl oz single cream
8 pink peppercorns
1 bouquet garni
150ml/5fl oz double cream
salt and freshly milled white pepper

Cut the lobster in half lengthways through the back, cutting from the tail through the shell. Discard the sac from the body, and pull the trail away. Reserve any spawn in a bowl. Crack the claw joints and the claws.

Melt the butter in the saucepan, then add all the lobster meat and shells, shallots, celeriac and carrot. Cook this slowly for 4 minutes, stirring continuously with a wooden spoon; do not let the butter colour. Add the brandy and set it alight. When the flames die down, stir in the vinegar and continue simmering for a further 2 minutes.

Remove the pan from the heat and stir in the flour and tomato purée. Cook over a low heat, stirring constantly, and gradually add the chicken stock, Madeira, cream and pink peppercorns.

Bring the sauce to the boil, stirring constantly, then adjust the seasoning and stir in the bouquet garni. Lower the heat and simmer for 35 minutes.

Remove the pieces of lobster and remove the meat from the shells. Crush any reserved lobster spawn and blend it into the sauce with the double cream. Simmer the sauce for 5 minutes. Pass the sauce through a coarse non-metallic sieve or muslin. Taste and adjust the seasoning.

VARIATIONS

American Shrimp Sauce or sauce aux cevettes Use the same ingredients and method as for lobster sauce but replace the lobster with 450g/1lb prawns.

Cardinal Sauce Use fish stock (pages 19–20) and béchamel sauce (page 26) with poached lobster and cayenne pepper.

Sauce Poulette Use mussels, adding cream and egg yolks, lemon juice and seasoning.

Mint Sauce

It is very important to use a very good-quality wine vinegar when making this, not malt vinegar. This is excellent served with spring lamb. *Makes about 6 tablespoons.*

2 large tablespoons finely chopped fresh mint
I tablespoon caster sugar
I tablespoon boiling water
2 tablespoons wine vinegar

Put the mint in a sauce boat with the sugar, then stir in the boiling water and allow to cool. Add the vinegar and allow it to infuse for at least 1 hour before serving.

Mushroom Sauce

Mary Jewry, in *Warnes Model Cookery Book* (1868), gave us this classical mushroom sauce for serving with chicken or rabbit, which takes about a quarter of an hour to make. I have not converted this beautiful recipe into modern text, simply because that would ruin it.

Mushroom Sauce for Chickens, &c.
One pint of young mushrooms;
one blade of mace; a little nutmeg and
salt; one ounce and a half of butter;
one pint of cream; a little flour.
Rub off the tender skin from about a
pint of young mushrooms, with a little
salt; then put them into a stewpan with
a blade of mace, a little grated nutmeg,
an ounce and a half of butter rolled in
a teaspoonful of flour, and a pint of
good cream. Put it over a clear fire,
and boil it up till sufficiently thick,
stirring it all the time; then pour it
round boiled fowls or rabbits.

Redcurrant Sauce

Serve this with game. *Makes about 100ml/ 4fl oz.*

 100g/4oz redcurrant jelly
 4 tablespoons port

Stir the jelly and port together in a saucepan over a medium heat and simmer for 3 minutes. Leave to cool, then cover and chill until required. Serve chilled.

Reform Sauce

Seventeenth-century recipes for this sauce specify using claret, but later recipes call for port, which is what I use today. Frenchman Alexis Soyer (1809–1858) invented this sauce in 1841, while he was chef at the Reform Club in London, in honour of the new kitchens that were installed there.

Charles Elmé Francatelli, who was the greatest chef I know of for copying other cook's recipes, claimed to invent this sauce as well when he was the chef at the Reform Club in 1852. Here is his version from *The Cook's Guide* (1869):

Prepare some Poivrade sauce 19 [refers to recipe 19 in his book] to this add a glass of port wine, half the quantity of Harvey, a teaspoon of Anchovy, and two good tablespoons of redcurrant jelly; boil together for five minutes, and pour into a clean small stewpan for use.

Here is an 1888 recipe from *Mrs Agnes B. Marshall's Cookery Book*:

Reforme Sauce for Cutlets. – One ounce of glaze, one wineglassful of claret or port, three quarters of a pint of brown sauce, the juice of one lemon, pinch of castor sugar, a few drops of Marshall's carmine, a dust of coralline pepper, and one large tablespoonful of red currant jelly; boil and keep skimmed till reduced a quarter part, then tammy and use.

Auguste Escoffier's recipe blends pepper and demi-glace sauces with julienned gherkins, a hard-boiled egg white, cooked mushrooms, a truffle and ox tongue, which is actually a direct copy of Alexis Soyer's 1841 recipe.

This is my version. The truffle is a wonderful addition but it is only optional, as it is so expensive. Serve this in the traditional way with lamb cutlets, or fillet of beef, pork or veal. *Makes about 225ml/8fl oz.*

 150ml/5fl oz pepper sauce (pages 37–8)
 150ml/5fl oz demi-glace sauce (page 35)
 1 tablespoon redcurrant jelly
 75g/3oz hard-boiled egg white,
 25g/1oz gherkin, cut into julienne strips
 25g/1oz mushroom, cut into julienne strips
 25g/1oz cooked ox tongue, cut into julienne strips
 25g/1 oz truffle (optional), cut into julienne strips

Place both sauces into saucepan over a high heat and bring to the boil, then lower the heat and leave to simmer for at least 20 minutes.

Skim the surface and stir in the redcurrant jelly, then return to the boil and boil for a further 3 minutes.

Add the egg white, gherkin, mushrooms, ox tongue and truffle.

Robert Sauce

Robert sauce, or *sauce Robert* as this is called in French, was one of the sauces from Dr William Kitchiner's period and it has an interesting, if inconclusive, history. A Mrs Mary Eaton includes a Robart sauce in *The Cook & Householder's Dictionary* of 1823, and Kitchiner lists Sauce Robert in *The Cook's Oracle* (1817).

Like other writers of old cookery books, Kitchiner attributed the origins of the sauce to a mysterious Frenchman with the name Robert. I presume he had in mind Robert l'Aine, under whom the legendary French chef Carême studied. Many years earlier, at the time of the Norman Conquest (1066), there had been a free exchange of languages and food between France and England, and although it was generally assumed this sauce was originally French, that was not the case. The French had their *brouet de chevreuil* (roebuck soup) and the English had their 'roebroth' or 'roebrewet', or roebuck, for which there were numerous varying 'receipes'. I suspect the French picked up one of these, and with the glorious faculty of altering names that they have, they thought its name must be the same as that of their famous Norman duke, so they called it Robert. In its original form 'Robert' was roebrewet, or roebuck sauce. It may be observed that roebuck is not once mentioned by the French writer Rabelais among the meats for which *sauce Robert* is necessary; modern taste has also abandoned roebuck, confining the choice of meat to pork and to goose.

Celebrated restaurateur Auguste Kettner did some research in the 1870s and he established that the sauce had, in fact, English origins, the name being a variant of 'roebrewet'. Kettner wrote in *Book of the Table* (1877) that the sauce was at least 300 years old then, but wasn't able to state exactly when it was first devised.

Kitchiner also provided the interesting information that one cookery book author of the period, Mary Smith (*c.*1772), called the sauce Roe-boat sauce, getting a little nearer to the original title than even Kitchiner had. That title is also similar to Mrs Eaton's Robart Sauce of 1823.

Old cookery books reveal many recipes for *sauce Robert*, and French cooks had a strong tendency to drench it with vinegar and wine, thus creating a distinctly sharp sauce. The recipe which I consider much the best is from restaurateur Antoine Beauvilliers, who is very chary of acid. Beauvilliers, credited with opening Paris' first restaurant in 1782 or 1786, cooked for many royal households. In 1814 he published two volumes of *L'Art du Cuisinier*. And now, my recipe, which I recommend with a fillet of pork or English black pudding. *Makes about 225ml/8fl oz.*

25g/1oz butter
100g/4oz onions or shallots, finely chopped
4 tablespoons lemon vinegar
300ml/10fl oz demi-glace sauce (page 35)
1 level tablespoon prepared English mustard
1 teaspoon finely chopped fresh parsley
salt and freshly milled black pepper

Melt the butter in a small saucepan over a medium heat, then add the onions or shallots and fry gently for 6 minutes, stirring occasionally. Add the lemon vinegar and continue cooking until it is absorbed.

Stir in the demi-glace sauce and simmer for a further 6 minutes, then blend in the mustard. Taste and adjust the seasoning. Sprinkle the parsley into the sauce.

VARIATION
Sauce Charcutière Simply add 25g/1oz sliced gherkins to Robert sauce. Serve with steaks.

Beauvilliers' Receipt for Sauce Robert

Cut six large onions or even more into dice, dredge them with flour, and pass them in butter till they are of a fine brown tint. Moisten them with a very little broth, and let them cook. Add salt, mignonette pepper, and last of all French mustard; after which it ought not to go to the fire, as to cook mustard spoils it. In lieu of French mustard use English mixed with tarragon vinegar.

Mrs Mary Eaton's *The Cook & Householder's Dictionary* (1823) gives the following recipe:

SAUCE ROBART. This is a favourite sauce for rump steaks, and is made in the following manner.

Put a piece of butter, the size of an egg, into a saucepan; and while browning over the fire, throw in a handful of sliced onions cut small. Fry them brown, but do not let them burn. Add half a spoonful of flour, shake the onions in it, and give it another fry. Then put in four spoonfuls of gravy, some pepper and salt, and boil it gently for ten minutes. Skim of the fat, add a teaspoonful of made mustard, a spoonful of vinegar, and the juice of half a lemon. Boil it all together, and pour it round the steaks, which should be a fine yellow brown, garnished with fried parsley and lemon.

Tartare Sauce

Breaded and fried plaice and scampi just wouldn't seem the same if this sauce hadn't been invented to serve with them. I also like to serve this with cold meat, poultry and game. *Makes about 350g/12 oz.*

3 hard-boiled eggs, shelled
1 raw egg yolk
300ml/10fl oz sunflower oil
1 tablespoon wine vinegar
1 teaspoon chopped fresh parsley
1 teaspoon snipped fresh chives
1 teaspoon finely chopped white part of a spring onion
1 teaspoon capers, well drained
large pinch of curry powder (pages 51–2)
1 tablespoon double cream
salt and freshly milled black pepper

Split the hard-boiled eggs and separate the whites and yolks. Rub the yolks through a fine sieve.

Beat in the raw yolk and season well. Add the sunflower oil, drop by drop, until the mixture emulsifies, then stir in the vinegar. Add the herbs, spring onions, capers, curry powder and cream. Taste and adjust the seasoning. Cover and chill until ready to serve. Serve chilled.

Wow-wow Sauce, A Sauce for Stewed or Bouilli Beef

I've taken this recipe for one of the most classical of English sauces from one of my previous books, *Dr William Kitchiner, A Regency Eccentric*. Dr Kitchiner excelled in inventing odd names for all types of food, with this being a typical example. He wrote: 'If you think (the above) is not sufficiently piquant, add to it some Capers, or minced Shallot, or one or two teaspoonsful of Wine Vinegar'.

I have taken the liberty, however, of adapting the original recipe to 20th-century tastes, including my meat stock recipe. I think this sauce goes exceeding well with boiled beef or a leg of lamb. *Makes about 300ml/10fl oz.*

100g/4oz brown roux (page 23)
300ml/10fl oz meat stock (pages 20–21), warm
1 tablespoon red wine vinegar
1 teaspoon prepared English mustard
1 tablespoon port
1 tablespoon finely chopped fresh parsley
6 pickled walnuts, diced

Place the roux in a large saucepan over a low heat and warm through until it softens. Gradually add the stock, stirring constantly to avoid any lumps. When the sauce is smooth and creamy, stir in the vinegar, mustard and port and simmer, stirring frequently, until the sauce is reduced to the consistency you want.

Add the parsley and the pickled walnuts, stirring for 1 minute. Taste and adjust the seasoning.

Mr Michael Kelly's Sauce for Tripe or Cow-heel or Calf's Head

Here is another of Dr Kitchiner's recipes from *The Cook's Oracle* (1817). Mr Michael Kelly was a composer and director of music at the Theatre Royal, Drury Lane, London, and the Italian Opera in 1823. He was also a very dear friend of Dr Kitchiner. In the original recipe, Kitchiner wrote: 'This sauce poured over sliced boiled beef, served with bubble and squeak or bangers and mash makes a nice change from expensive cuts of meat.'

INGREDIENTS:
Garlic Vinegar 1 tablespoonful; mustard; brown sugar; and black pepper;
1 teaspoonful each; oiled butter ½ pint.
1. Mix the dry ingredients with the vinegar; and 2. Stir into the hot oiled butter.

International and Modern Sauces

America

I spent nearly a year living and travelling around America – from Chinatown in San Francisco to Sioux City, Denver, New Orleans, Philadelphia and Boston – and I picked up quite a few recipes along the way, including these wonderful sauces that I am going to share with you now.

All-American Tomato Sauce

Here is my cousin Lee Bridge Cognetta's favourite sauce. *Makes about 250ml/9fl oz.*

    6 tablespoons olive oil
    I onion, thinly sliced
    2 garlic cloves, crushed
    700g/1½lb fresh plum tomatoes, peeled, seeded
        and finely chopped, or tinned tomatoes, well
        drained
    2 tablespoons finely chopped fresh basil
    I teaspoon brown sugar
    100g/4oz tomato purée
    salt and freshly milled black pepper

Heat the olive oil in a large saucepan over a medium heat. Add the onion and garlic and fry for 3 minutes. Stir in the tomatoes, basil, sugar, salt and pepper and simmer for 20 minutes, stirring occasionally.

Blend in the tomato purée and simmer for a further 12 minutes. Taste and adjust the seasoning.

VARIATION

Texas Tomato Sauce Add 2 tablespoons finely chopped seeded green chillies and 1 tablespoon chilli powder. This is excellent with steaks, especially the rib-eyes, boneless pieces of steak cut from the rib section.

Chicken on Her Nest

Roast a chicken until there are only 25 minutes of roasting time left. Meanwhile, boil 450g/1lb wild rice until it is tender and hard boil 6 eggs.

Place the well-drained cooked rice on a large ovenproof serving dish with the shelled, whole eggs on the rice. Place the chicken on the rice, pour over the all-American tomato sauce (above) and return the dish to an oven pre-heated to 180°C/350°F/gas mark 4 for the final 25 minutes roasting time until the chicken is cooked through and the juices run clear when you pierce the thigh with the tip of a knife. Garnish with fresh parsley. *Serves 4.*

Californian Sherry Sauce

Try this with veal kidneys – I guarantee you won't be disappointed. *Makes about 200ml/ 7fl oz.*

> 25g/1oz butter
> 2 tablespoons olive oil
> 75g/3oz diced raw ham
> 1 garlic clove, crushed
> 4 shallots, chopped
> 150ml/5fl oz dry sherry
> 150ml/5fl oz demi-glace sauce (page 35)
> salt and freshly milled black pepper

Melt the butter with the olive oil in a saucepan over a medium heat. Add the ham, garlic and shallots and fry for 4 minutes, stirring frequently. Add the sherry and boil until the mixture reduces by half.

Season and stir in the demi-glace sauce and simmer for 6 minutes. Taste and adjust the seasoning.

Cider Sauce for Baked Ham

I was given two recipes for a sauce to accompany baked ham while I was travelling across America. This one from Pennsylvania is made with cider, and the other – believe it or not – is made with Coca-Cola. Not surprisingly, I prefer this one. *Makes about 300ml/10fl oz.*

> 600ml/1 pint medium-sweet cider
> 75g/3oz seedless raisins
> 6 cloves
> 1 bay leaf
> pinch of grated nutmeg
> 150ml/5fl oz velouté sauce (page 26)
> salt and freshly milled black pepper

Place the cider, raisins, cloves, bay leaf and nutmeg in a saucepan and boil until the cider reduces by half. Pass the sauce through a fine sieve, then return it to the pan. Stir in the velouté sauce and simmer for 4 minutes. Taste and adjust the seasoning.

VARIATION
Champagne Sauce Use the same ingredients and method as for the cider sauce, but replace the cider with Champagne, and add 2 tablespoons double cream and 25g/1oz melted butter with the velouté sauce. Serve this with oysters, ham, game or pork.

Hot Creole Sauce

Serve this sauce with steaks, chicken and hamburgers. *Makes about 300ml/10 fl oz.*

> 2 tablespoons olive oil
> 25g/1oz butter
> 2 garlic cloves, crushed
> 2 chillies, seeded and chopped
> 6 shallots, finely chopped
> 2 beef tomatoes, seed and diced
> 1 celery stick, finely chopped
> 2 tablespoons chicken stock (page 21)
> 150ml/5fl oz red wine, such as claret
> 1 teaspoon Worcestershire sauce
> 1 teaspoon chopped fresh parsley
> pinch each of fresh oregano, thyme and tarragon
> 1 tablespoon Tabasco sauce
> 1 teaspoon cayenne pepper
> 150ml/5fl oz Espagnole sauce (pages 38–9)
> salt and freshly milled black pepper

Melt the butter with the oil in a large saucepan, add the garlic, chillies and shallots and fry for 1 minute, stirring frequently. Add the rest of the ingredients, except the Espagnole sauce, and bring to the boil, stirring constantly. Lower the heat and simmer for 30 minutes, stirring frequently. Stir in the Espagnole sauce and continue to simmer for a further 15 minutes. Taste and adjust the seasoning.

Hot and Spicy Green Tomato Sauce

I like to serve this with all barbecued meat and fish. You will find that the flavour of hot chillies and the tartness of the lime and green tomatoes combine to give a boost to any party. *Makes about 225ml/8fl oz.*

2 tablespoons olive oil
2 garlic cloves, crushed
6 shallots, finely chopped
8 green tomatoes, skinned and finely chopped
3 chillies, seeded and finely chopped
150ml/5fl oz red wine vinegar
2 tablespoons brown sugar
finely grated rind and juice of 1 lime
2 teaspoons Tabasco sauce
1 teaspoon grated fresh root ginger
salt and freshly milled black pepper

Heat the oil in a saucepan over a medium heat, add the garlic, shallots, tomatoes and chillies and fry for about 4 minutes, stirring frequently. Add the remaining ingredients and bring to the boil, then lower the heat and simmer for 15 minutes.

Purée the sauce in a blender or food processor for 20 seconds. Taste and adjust the seasoning.

Oyster Sauce

Food is a much more significant in my life than simply as a means of survival. In fact, without good food I do not think I could survive. And one of the best ways to enhance any food is to serve it with a sauce. This recipe is very special, and it qualifies as one of the best among those I consider to be excellent sauces. I first came across it in Chinatown in San Francisco. Serve it with lamb fillet or leg. *Makes about 200ml/7fl oz.*

12 fresh oysters
juice of 1 lemon
25g/1oz butter, softened and blended with
25g/1oz plain flour
1 teaspoon soy sauce
1 teaspoon Worcestershire sauce
pinch of cayenne pepper
freshly grated nutmeg
150ml/5fl oz sour cream

Open the oysters over a fine sieve over a saucepan to collect all the juice; set aside the oysters. Add the lemon juice to the oyster juice and bring to the boil, then add the butter and flour mixture, a little at a time (you may not need all of it) to thicken the sauce.

Stir in the soy and Worcestershire sauces, a large pinch of cayenne pepper and a little nutmeg. Add the oysters and simmer the sauce for 30 seconds, then very slowly add the sour cream. Heat through and serve.

VARIATION

Millionaires' Oyster Sauce Add 50g/2oz smoked salmon, cut into small diamond shapes and sprinkle the finished sauce with 25g/1oz Beluga caviar and fine strips of truffle. For a snack fit for a millionaire, serve with brown bread and butter, garnished with a bottle of chilled Champagne.

Pacific Prawn Sauce

A whole poached salmon always looks impressive, but even more so when you garnish it with some fresh parsley and have a little of this pale pink sauce poured along its edges, with the remaining sauce in a sauce boat. Also, like many of the other sauces throughout this book, you can also use it for a fondue. *Makes about 450ml/15fl oz.*

> 300ml/10fl oz fish velouté sauce (page 26)
> 150ml/5fl oz sour cream
> 1 tablespoon tomato purée
> 225g/8oz raw large prawns, such as tiger prawns, chopped
> cayenne pepper
> 1 tablespoon finely chopped fresh parsley
> 2 tablespoons rose petal vinegar (page 16), or your favourite vinegar
> 6 cooked tiger or king prawns, shelled and left whole
> salt and freshly milled black pepper
> fresh parsley sprigs, to garnish

Place the fish velouté sauce in a saucepan over a medium heat. Blend together the sour cream and tomato puree, then slowly add it to the velouté sauce, stirring constantly.

Add the chopped prawns, a pinch of cayenne pepper, the chopped parsley and salt and pepper. Simmer for 5 minutes, then stir in the vinegar and whole prawns just before serving. Taste and adjust the seasoning. Garnish with fresh parsley sprigs.

Pacific Pineapple Sauce

Served with swordfish steaks along the Pacific coast, this sauce also goes well with grilled tuna and halibut. *Makes about 225g/8oz.*

> 2 tablespoons peanut oil
> 2 garlic cloves, crushed
> 6 shallots, finely chopped
> 1 small fresh pineapple, peeled and diced
> 2 tablespoons brown sugar
> 2 tablespoons white wine vinegar
> generous pinch each of fresh thyme, ground cloves and ground allspice
> 150ml/5fl oz white sauce (page 25)
> 50g/2oz unsalted butter, softened
> salt and freshly milled black pepper

Heat the oil in a saucepan over a medium heat, add the garlic and shallots and fry for 2 minutes, stirring often. Add the pineapple and continue cooking for a further 5 minutes, still stirring occasionally.

Stir in the sugar, vinegar, herbs and spices and simmer, stirring constantly, for 10 minutes.

Add the white sauce and the butter and continue simmering over a low heat for 8 minutes, stirring all the time. Taste and adjust the seasoning.

VARIATION

Sweet and Sour Sauce Add thinly sliced red, green and yellow peppers and thinly sliced baby sweetcorn with the garlic and shallots, then add 3 tablespoons extra vinegar and 4 tablespoons white wine. This sauce compliments grilled king prawns, pork or chicken

Paradise Sauce

This is one of the richest sauce in Creole cookery, and Madeira is the only wine that should be used. I think this is a perfect sauce to serve with quail and duckling. *Makes about 300ml/10fl oz.*

> 50g/2oz butter
> 50g/2oz plain flour
> 600ml/1 pint meat stock (pages 20–21), hot
> 300ml/10fl oz Madeira
> 2 tablespoons redcurrant jelly
> 1 tablespoon raspberry vinegar
> 100g/oz fresh redcurrants, rinsed and stalks removed
> 25g/1oz truffle, sliced (optional)
> salt and freshly milled black pepper

Melt the butter in a large saucepan over a low heat. Add the flour, stirring until smooth, and cook for about 12 minutes until it becomes light in colour and crumbly in texture like a blond roux (page 23). Slowly stir in the meat stock and bring to the boil, then lower the heat and simmer for 15 minutes.

Add the Madeira, redcurrant jelly and vinegar, stirring until the jelly dissolves, then continue simmering for a further 15 minutes.

Stir in the fresh redcurrants and truffle and continue simmering for a further 4 minutes. Taste and adjust the seasoning.

VARIATION

Carib Paradise Island Sauce Use the same ingredients and method as for the paradise sauce, but add the seeds and juice from 4 passion fruits, 4 tablespoons coconut cream, 1 thinly sliced mango and 12 thinly sliced seedless black grapes when you add the Madeira. Simmer the sauce for a further 10 minutes, then strain. Taste and adjust the seasoning. I like to serve this with boiled ham or boiled leg of lamb.

Prune Sauce

Californians enjoy this served with wild boar steaks or sucking pig. *Makes about 300g/10oz.*

> 225g/8oz ready-to-eat stoned prunes
> pinch of ground cinnamon
> 1 tablespoon port
> 4–5 tablespoons lemon juice
> 1 tablespoon redcurrant jelly
> 250ml/9fl oz Espagnole sauce (pages 38–9)

Put the prunes, cinnamon, port, lemon juice and redcurrant jelly into a saucepan over a high heat and bring to the boil, then lower the heat and simmer for 2 minutes, stirring occasionally.

Stir in the Espagnole sauce and continue simmering for a further 5 minutes.

San Francisco Barbecue Sauce

Use this versatile sauce to baste foods while they are barbecuing or grilling, or use it to impart a barbecued flavour to foods roasting in the oven. *Makes about 300ml/10fl oz.*

150ml/5fl oz olive oil
2 garlic cloves, crushed
150ml/5fl oz dry sherry
3 tablespoons tomato purée
225g/8oz tomatoes, peeled, seeded and finely
   chopped
1 tablespoons chopped fresh basil
½ teaspoon Tabasco sauce
2 tablespoons honey
1 teaspoon ground ginger
juice of 1 lemon
4 tablespoons soy sauce
salt and freshly milled black pepper

Blend all the ingredients together. Rub the sauce into a duckling before roasting or pour it over chicken or spare ribs in an ovenproof dish and roast at 160°C/325°F/gas mark 3 for 35–40 minutes.

White Wine, Honey and Garlic Marinade . . . and Sauce

Here is what I consider to be a typical American marinade that also doubles as a sauce. If you are preparing this to serve with chicken, pork or lamb, marinate the meat for 4 hours in it before you cook it.

I must emphasize again that cheap wine should not be used in sauces or marinades because it does adversely affects the overall flavour. *Makes about 225ml/8fl oz.*

300ml/10fl oz good-quality white wine, such as
   Chardonnay
150g/5oz clear honey
150ml/5fl oz olive oil
4 garlic cloves, crushed
1 teaspoon fennel seeds, crushed
2 bay leaves
1 teaspoon coriander seeds, crushed
2 tablespoons finely chopped fresh parsley
1 teaspoon dry thyme
150ml/5fl oz velouté sauce (page 26)
salt and freshly milled black pepper

To use as a marinade, combine all the ingredients, except the velouté sauce, in a large non-metallic bowl and mix together. Add the meat and marinate, then use the marinade to baste the main ingredient while it cooks.

To use as a sauce, put all the marinade ingredients, except the velouté sauce, in a saucepan over a high heat and boil until reduced by half. Pass through a fine non-metallic sieve, then return it to the rinsed-out pan. Add the velouté sauce and simmer for a further 4 minutes. Taste and adjust the seasoning. Serve with the meat of your choice.

Australia

The Australians use sauces that are derived from many different cultures. Here are two recipes from my cousins, Doreen and Shirley Morton, who live in Nangwary, South Australia.

Lemon Grass, Orange and Coconut Sauce

Serve this with sliced duck breast or any lightly flavoured game. *Makes about 350ml/12fl oz.*

I tablespoon olive oil
I tablespoon chopped fresh lemon grass
I tablespoon grated fresh ginger
2 garlic cloves, crushed
I fresh red chilli, seeded and chopped
150ml/5fl oz freshly squeezed orange juice
150ml/5fl oz coconut cream
150ml/5fl oz velouté sauce (page 26)
I tablespoon chopped fresh coriander
salt and freshly milled black pepper

Heat the olive oil in a large saucepan, add the lemon grass, ginger, garlic and chilli and fry for 4 minutes, stirring frequently.

Stir in the orange juice, coconut cream and velouté sauce and bring to the boil, then lower the heat and simmer for 5 minutes, stirring occasionally. Sprinkle with fresh coriander. Taste and adjust the seasoning.

Hake with Fresh Herb, Tomato and Wine Sauce

I suggest using hake in this but you can also make it with your favourite fish. *Serves 4.*

450g/1 lb hake fillets
50g/2oz butter
3 tablespoons extra virgin olive oil
4 shallots
I garlic clove, crushed
6 tomatoes, chopped
2 tablespoons tomato purée
2 sprigs each of fresh tarragon, thyme, parsley and rosemary
300ml/10fl oz dry white wine, such as a Chardonnay
150ml/5fl oz velouté sauce (page 26)
salt and freshly milled black pepper
chopped fresh tarragon and parsley, to garnish

Preheat the oven to a very low setting. Season the fish lightly. Melt half the butter with the oil in a large frying pan and sauté the fish for 3 minutes, then transfer it to a warm serving plate and keep warm. Add the shallots and garlic to the pan and sauté slowly for 3 minutes.

Add the tomatoes, tomato purée, herbs and wine and bring to the boil, then lower the heat and simmer for 15 minutes. Stir in the velouté sauce, season and continue simmering for a further 10 minutes.

Pass the sauce through a fine non-metallic sieve and return it to the rinsed-out pan. Add the fish and simmer until the fish is cooked through and flakes easily when tested with the tip of a knife. Stir in the remaining butter and taste and adjust the seasoning. Garnish with the chopped herbs.

Austria

Austria is famous for several sauces, including caper and dill, but other 'national' sauces reflect the influence of Germany, Hungary and Italy. The individuality of the cuisine is reflected in its use of goose fat, rather than butter, in roux and some sauces.

Dill Sauce

Dill is very popular in Austria and is extensively used as a flavouring to sauces. Add 1 tablespoon chopped fresh dill to butter sauce (page 29) just before it is served. Serve with fish.

Kren Sauce

This is an Austrian version of horseradish sauce that is served hot with roast beef. Put 2 tablespoons meat stock (pages 20–21) into a small saucepan and bring to the boil. Add 1 tablespoon fresh white breadcrumbs and mix together well, then blend in 1 tablespoon grated fresh horseradish, 3 tablespoons sour cream and a pinch of saffron. Simmer for 2 minutes and it is ready to serve. *Makes about 150ml/5fl oz.*

Mackerel with Horseradish Sauce

This is one of the simplest of Austrian dishes, with the horseradish (*kren*) making the sauce also suitable for serving with pork, ox tail, fish salads and any game, as well as mackerel. If you want a richer sauce, add extra butter at the end of the cooking process with a little double cream. *Serves 4.*

4 mackerel fillets, cleaned, seasoned and grilled

for the horseradish sauce
25g/1oz goose fat or butter
25g/1oz plain flour
300ml/10fl oz sour cream, warmed
2 tablespoons grated fresh horseradish
1 tablespoon white wine vinegar
pinch of paprika
pinch of salt

To make the sauce, melt the fat in a large saucepan over a low heat. Add the flour, stir until it is smooth and cook for about 12 minutes until it becomes light in colour and crumbly in texture like a blond roux (page 23).

Slowly stir in the warm sour cream, stirring well, then add the remaining ingredients. Stir well and allow the sauce to simmer for 8 minutes. Taste and adjust the seasoning. Serve with the mackerel.

VARIATION
Honey, Mustard and Poppy Seed Sauce I created this sauce using the above recipe, but stirred in the following ingredients at the very end of the cooking process: 2 tablespoons clear honey, 2 tablespoons prepared English mustard, 1 tablespoon poppy seeds and freshly milled black pepper. This is excellent to serve with chicken and pork.

Belgium

Sauce Roeselare, Francis Carroll Style

I do not have a great deal of knowledge of Belgian sauces, but my friend and fellow chef, Francis Carroll, certainly does. Francis was born in Roeselare and his family, like most families from that area, ate chicken regularly. It's one of Belgium's national foods and is justly famed for its high quality. *Makes about 300ml/10fl oz.*

    I quantity *beurre blanc* (page 29)
    100g/4oz wild mushrooms
    I tablespoon chestnut purée, blended with
      4 tablespoons full-flavoured chicken stock
      (page 21)
    2 egg yolks
    225ml/8fl oz crème fraîche
    2 tablespoons finely chopped fresh tarragon
    salt and freshly milled black pepper

Make up the *beurre blanc* recipe, adding the wild mushrooms, chestnut purée and chicken stock when you add the shallots.

Put the egg yolks into a mixing bowl and whisk in the crème fraîche. Slowly add half the *beurre blanc*, whisking vigorously.

Pour the sauce into a saucepan over a low heat and stir constantly until it thickens. Taste and adjust the seasoning. Serve with chicken.

Add the tarragon to the remaining *beurre blanc* to make an accompanying sauce. Spoon the sauces on the plate to make the appearance of a pinwheel out of the contrasting colours.

Caribbean

As the sun sets on every beach in the West Indies, locals sit waiting for the embers in their beach fires to smoulder white so that they can barbecue their evening meal. Chances are they will be using one of these sauces, each one bursting with the flavours of the Tropics.

Mango and Papaya Sauce

Similar to a sweet and sour sauce, this West Indian recipe is served with vegetables, fish and chicken wings. *Makes about 225ml/8fl oz.*

    2 tablespoons olive oil
    3 garlic cloves, very finely chopped
    1 mango, peeled, stone removed and diced
    1 papaya, peeled, seeded and diced
    6 shallots
    150ml/5fl oz red wine vinegar
    50g/2oz brown sugar
    50g/2oz raisins
    50g/2oz sultanas
    3 garlic cloves, crushed
    2 teaspoons grated fresh root ginger
    pinch each of ground cinnamon, ground allspice
      and dry thyme
    150ml/5fl oz Espagnole sauce (pages 38–9)
    freshly milled black pepper

Heat the olive oil in a saucepan over a medium heat, add the garlic, mango, papaya and shallots and cook for 3 minutes, stirring all the time.

Add all the remaining ingredients, except the Espagnole sauce, and bring to the boil, then lower the heat and simmer for 15 minutes. Stir in the Espagnole sauce, a little at a time, until the sauce is smooth. Simmer for 5 minutes, then taste and adjust the seasoning.

Papaya Sauce

For a meal out of the ordinary, try this exotic sauce with wild boar steaks, or, if you are not feeling that adventurous, grilled pork chops. If the sauce isn't as thick as you like after it simmers, stir in 1 tablespoon of butter and flour mashed together and continue simmering until it thickens. *Makes about 350ml/12fl oz.*

    1 large ripe papaya, peeled, seeded and chopped
    1 tablespoon honey
    1 tablespoon grated fresh root ginger
    2 tablespoon red wine vinegar
    1 teaspoon ground allspice
    300ml/10fl oz chicken stock (page 21)
    grated rind and juice of 1 lime
    150ml/5fl oz velouté sauce (page 26), warm

Put all the ingredients, except the velouté sauce, in a saucepan over a high heat and bring to the boil, then lower the heat and simmer for 20 minutes.

Pass the stock through a fine non-metallic sieve into the velouté sauce and bring to the boil, then lower the heat and simmer for a further 20 minutes.

Papaya Mustard Sauce

Believe it or not, this is a tasty accompaniment to traditional English black pudding, especially if you add an extra tablespoon of Dijon mustard. Marinate spare ribs in this sauce overnight, sprinkle with freshly ground black pepper, and roast in the oven or, better still, over a barbecue for a flavour you will never forget.

This will keep for up to 3 days in a sealed container in the refrigerator, and is also good for serving with chicken and fish. *Makes about 300ml/10fl oz.*

2 tablespoons olive oil
1 garlic clove, crushed
6 shallots, finely chopped
1 papaya, peeled, seeded and diced
150ml/5fl oz red wine vinegar
3 tablespoons prepared English mustard
1 tablespoon brown sugar
2 teaspoons Worcestershire sauce
1 teaspoon Tabasco sauce
pinch each of ground allspice and fresh thyme
150ml/5fl oz Espagnole sauce (pages 38–9)
freshly milled black pepper

Heat the oil in a saucepan over a medium heat, add the garlic and shallots and fry for 2 minutes, stirring frequently. Add the remaining ingredients, except the Espagnole sauce, and bring to the boil, lower the heat and simmer for 15 minutes. Slowly whisk in the Espagnole sauce and continue simmering the sauce for 10 minutes. Taste and adjust the seasoning.

Sofrito Sauce

A Spanish West Indian sauce to serve with pork, beef, chicken or vegetables. Pernod provides the flavour of aniseed and a vibrant yellow, and salt pork adds flavour. *Makes about 75ml/3fl oz.*

25g/1oz butter
100g/4oz salt pork, diced
2 garlic cloves, crushed
6 shallots, finely chopped
1 red or green pepper, seeded and finely chopped
2 beef tomatoes, skinned and diced
2 tablespoons chicken stock (page 21)
1 tablespoon Pernod
pinch of turmeric
freshly milled black pepper

Melt the butter in a saucepan over a medium heat, add the salt pork and fry for about 10 minutes. Remove the pork pieces and discard, leaving the flavoured fat behind in the pan.

Add the garlic, shallots, pepper and tomatoes and cook over a medium heat for about 10 minutes, stirring occasionally.

Add the chicken stock, Pernod, turmeric and pepper and simmer for about 5 minutes. Taste and adjust the seasoning; you probably will not need any salt because of the salty pork.

Sweet and Sour Pineapple Sauce

You will find this is very different from the Chinese versions of sweet and sour sauce, and I think it can be served with every type of food except game. This recipe reflects the Caribbeans' knack of combining the islands' plentiful wild fruits into exciting sauces to serve with their many fish and wild pig dishes. Use your favourite fruit to replace the pineapple to create your own variation. *Makes about 225g/8oz.*

25g/1oz butter
25g/1oz each of green, red and yellow peppers, julienned
6 shallots, thinly sliced
½ fresh pineapple, peeled and julienned
25g/1oz plain flour, seasoned with salt and freshly milled black pepper
150ml/5fl oz fresh pineapple juice, warm
4 tablespoons white wine vinegar
1 tablespoon soy sauce
red berries
ground cinnamon

Melt the butter in a saucepan over a medium heat, add the peppers and shallots and fry for 4 minutes, stirring frequently. Add the pine-apple and continue cooking for a further 2 minutes. Sprinkle with seasoned flour and cook for 2 minutes. Slowly stir in the pineapple juice, stirring until the sauce is smooth. Add the vinegar and soy sauce and simmer over a low heat for 3 minutes. Sprinkle with red berries and ground cinnamon before serving.

China

Out of all the seemingly endless recipes for Chinese sauces, I have choosen six which I think will enhance a variety of menus.

Black Bean Sauce

Serve this traditional Chinese sauce with stir-fried chicken, pork or beef. If you don't plan to use it immediately, it will keep for up to a week in the fridge. Add it to stir-frying meat just before the meat finishes cooking, but with enough time to heat the sauce through. *Makes about 350ml/12fl oz.*

    4 tablespoons fermented black beans
    1 tablespoon peanut oil
    3 spring onions, chopped
    1 garlic clove, chopped
    2.5cm/1in piece fresh root ginger, peeled and
      sliced
    2 tablespoons dark soy sauce
    2 tablespoons cream sherry
    1 teaspoon brown sugar
    300ml/10fl oz water
    1 tablespoon sesame oil

Place the beans in a colander and let cold water run over them for at least 5 minutes, making sure they are thoroughly rinsed to remove the saltiness.

Heat the oil in a saucepan or wok over a medium heat, add the onions, garlic and ginger and stir-fry for 2 minutes. Add all the remaining ingredients, except the sesame oil, and simmer for 20 minutes, stirring occasionally.

Pass the sauce through a fine sieve and stir in the sesame oil. Leave to cool and use as required.

La Fu Jiang

Keep this sauce in the refrigerator for several weeks, ready to heat up and serve with your favourite cut of pork, or, pour it over the meat and then roast it at 220°C/425°F/gas mark 7 for 25 minutes per 450g/1lb. *Makes 225ml/8fl oz.*

    3 tablespoons peanut oil
    2 spring onions, finely chopped
    1 teaspoon grated fresh root ginger
    1 tablespoon bean curd
    50g/2oz canned bamboo shoots, well drained
    75g/3oz wild mushrooms
    3 tablespoons hoisin sauce
    2 tablespoons red wine vinegar
    1 tablespoon light soy sauce
    1 tablespoon cornflour mixed with 1 tablespoon
      dry sherry
    150ml/5fl oz chicken stock (page 21)

Heat the oil in a large frying pan or wok over a medium heat, add the onions, ginger and bean curd and stir-fry for 1 minute. Stir in the remaining ingredients and simmer for 25 minutes.

Lung Ha Jiang

This sauce goes particularly well with shellfish, sea bass and red snapper. *Makes about 250ml/9fl oz.*

2 tablespoons peanut oil
2 garlic cloves, crushed
1 teaspoon grated fresh root ginger
1 teaspoon brown sugar
2 tablespoons white wine vinegar
2 tablespoons light soy sauce
1 tablespoon dry sherry
300ml/10fl oz fish stock (pages 19–20)
150ml/5fl oz fish velouté sauce (page 26)

Heat the oil in a large saucepan or wok over a medium heat, add the garlic and ginger and stir-fry for 30 seconds, stirring occasionally. Stir in the sugar, vinegar, soy sauce, sherry and fish stock and bring to the boil, then lower the heat and simmer for 45 minutes or until the sauce reduces by half.

Skim the surface to remove any fat. Stir in the velouté sauce and continue simmering for 20 minutes.

Cho Low Yu

This recipe for lemon sole in with sweet and sour sauce is an ideal dinner party dish. I like to serve it with broccoli or mange tout with Chinese noodles. *Serves 4.*

2 tablespoons sesame oil
3 garlic cloves, crushed
25g/1oz cucumber, finely sliced
25g/1oz pickled onions, finely sliced
25g/1oz onions, finely sliced
1 teaspoon grated fresh root ginger
finely grated rind and juice of 1 lemon
150ml/5fl oz white wine vinegar
3 tablespoons brown sugar
2 tablespoons soy sauce
150ml/5fl oz cheese sauce (pages 25–6)
450g/1lb lemon sole fillets, skinned
lemon slices and parsley, to garnish

Preheat the oven to 220°C/425°F/gas mark 7. Heat the sesame oil in a large frying pan or wok, add the garlic and stir-fry for 30 seconds. Add all the remaining ingredients, except the cheese sauce and lemon sole fillets, and stir well to dissolve the sugar. Bring to the boil, then lower the heat and simmer until the mixture is reduced by half.

Stir in the cheese sauce and continue simmering for a further 20 minutes. Roll up the lemon sole fillets with their skinned side out and secure with wooden cocktail sticks. Arrange the fillets in a single layer in an ovenproof dish, cover with the sauce and bake for 15 to 20 minutes until the flesh flakes easily when tested with the tip of a knife.

Remove the dish from the oven and place the fillets on a warm, dark serving dish and remove the wooden sticks. Cover with the sauce and garnish with a few slices of fresh lemon and parsley for a striking presentation.

Ngo Pa Tsup

I found the original 19th-century recipe for this sauce, designed to serve with steak, very bland, so I revised it for the 20th-century tastes. Stir-fried pieces of sirloin or fillet steak, cooked in peanut oil with ginger and garlic, with a little of this sauce poured over and fried for a further, 5 minutes will give you a true flavour of the Orient. *Makes about 300ml/10fl oz.*

3 tablespoons peanut oil
3 garlic cloves, crushed
1 teaspoon grated fresh root ginger
8 shallots, thinly sliced
1 teaspoon light soy sauce
150ml/5fl oz meat stock (pages 20–21; made with beef)
2 tablespoons red wine vinegar
2 tablespoons medium sherry
2 tablespoons oyster sauce (page 61)
300ml/10fl oz Bordelaise sauce (page 35)
8 shallots, thinly sliced, to garnish

Heat the oil in a large frying pan or wok over a medium heat, add the garlic, ginger and shallots and sauté for 4 minutes, stirring frequently. Add all the remaining ingredients, except the Bordelaise sauce. Bring to the boil, then lower the heat and boil until the sauce is reduced by half.

Skim the surface to remove any fat and stir in the Bordelaise sauce. Simmer for at least 35 minutes. Add sliced shallots just before serving.

Op Tsup

The original version of this Cantonese recipe is more than 100 years old, but, yet again, I have added extra ingredients to make it tastier. This sauce can be used either to baste the duck before cooking or it can be served in a sauce boat to accompany the portioned duck.

In a sauce such as this, which is intended to serve with duck, which is such a rich meat, I think my technique of adding vinegar really comes into its own. During the cooking process, the vinegar helps to modify the richness. *Makes about 225ml/8fl oz.*

150ml/5fl oz game stock (page 22)
3 shallots, finely chopped
50g/2oz walnuts, crushed
3 tablespoons orange and green peppercorn vinegar (page 15)
grated rind and juice of 2 large oranges
3 tablespoons soy sauce
150ml/5fl oz plum sauce
salt and freshly milled black pepper

Place all the ingredients, except the plum sauce, in a large frying pan or wok over a high heat and boil until the liquids are reduced by half.

Pass the stock through a fine non-metallic sieve, then return to rinsed-out pan.

Stir in the plum sauce and return to the boil, then lower the heat and simmer for at least 20 minutes. Taste and adjust the seasoning.

England

Nut Sauce

Here is my version of the French *sauce noisette*, which I serve with fresh Dover sole. I cooked this for a dinner at Wembley Stadium in London in 1987, attended by HRH The Prince of Wales, and he described this as 'a French sauce under an English master'. *Makes about 175ml/6fl oz.*

50g/2oz blanched almonds
1 tablespoon honey, warmed
25g/1oz butter, softened
150ml/5fl oz Hollandaise sauce (page 31)
1 tablespoon snipped fresh chives

Toast the almonds lightly under a grill, then crush them finely and blend them with the honey and butter.

Warm the Hollandaise sauce in the top of a double boiler or in a heatproof bowl sitting over a pan of gently simmering water. Slowly stir in the almond-butter mixture until completely blended together. Sprinkle with chives and taste and adjust the seasoning. Pour along the side of the fish, serving the remainder in a sauce boat.

Port and Pink Peppercorn Sauce

This is one of my original recipes, and I like to serve it with roast ducking. *Makes about 300ml/10fl oz.*

600ml/1 pint perfect gravy (pages 44–5)
6 tablespoons port
10 pink peppercorns
150ml/5fl oz double cream

Put the gravy in a saucepan over a high heat and boil until it is reduced by half. Stir in the port and peppercorns and simmer the sauce for 5 minutes. Do not let the sauce come to the boil or you will lose the flavour of the port. Stir in the double cream just before serving.

VARIATION

Rose Petal and Honey Sauce for Wild Breast of Duckling I get many requests to cook this unique sauce when I make guest appearance at hotels and restaurants throughout the UK. Simply add 2 tablespoons rose petal vinegar (page 16) and 2 tablespoons honey to the port and pink peppercorn sauce. Do not pour the sauce over the duck breast. Instead, place it in the bowl of the plate and put the sliced duck breast on the sauce. Sprinkle with rose petals and fresh mint leaves for a stunning effect.

Royal Lamb Korma

I am a great fan of the Gaylord Indian restaurant in Manchester, where the tandoori ovens are on the go day and night baking naan, chapati and paratha breads. The chefs are usually reluctant to give away their secret recipes, but they kindly gave me this classic sauce for *shahi korma. Serves 6.*

2 tablespoons olive oil
8 green cardamom pods
6 cloves
2.5cm/1in cinnamon stick
175g/6oz shallots, finely chopped
1 teaspoon coriander seeds
1 tablespoon ground cumin
pinch of turmeric
300ml/10fl oz double cream
freshly milled black paper
1.1kg/2½lb lean lamb, such as leg or neck fillet, trimmed and cubed

for the creamy almond sauce
6 cloves of garlic, crushed
1 teaspoon grated fresh root ginger
75g/3oz blanched almonds, chopped
150ml/5fl oz meat stock (pages 20–21)

Preheat the oven to 200°C/400°F/gas mark 6.

Put the garlic, ginger, almonds and meat stock for the almond sauce in a blender or food processor, or use a pestle and mortar, and blend into a paste; set aside.

Put the olive oil, cardamom pods, cloves, cinnamon stick, shallots, coriander seeds, cumin and turmeric in a blender or food processor, or use a pestle and mortar, and grind together. Place this mixture in a large saucepan over a medium heat and cook for about 5 minutes. Stir in the reserved paste and simmer for a further 5 minutes over a low heat, stirring occasionally.

Stir in the cream and pepper and continue simmering for 20 minutes, stirring constantly.

Add the almond stock liquid and cook for a further 5 minutes on a low heat.

Add the freshly milled black pepper, cream and cayenne and simmer for 20 minutes, stirring all the time.

Place cubes of lamb in an ovenproof dish, cover with the sauce and cook for 1 hour.

Stilton Sauce

This is another of my original recipes, which I serve with chicken or steaks. Or I suggest you try this poured over a vegetable bake, sprinkled with breadcrumbs, with a medium-rare steak, or with cauliflower and new potatoes.

Without doubt, Stilton is the king of English cheeses, and the ideal choice with which to end an enjoyable evening meal. Whenever any of my friends want to win me over (please give them a copy of this), a nice baby Stilton and a bottle of vintage port does it every time. *Makes about 550ml/18fl oz.*

600ml/1 pint white sauce (page 25)
3 tablespoons aged port
75g/3oz Stilton cheese, crumbled.
2 tablespoons of good meat glaze
6 mushrooms, very finely chopped
1 tablespoon mushroom ketchup
50g/2oz best-quality butter
salt and freshly milled black pepper
finely shredded fresh mint and parsley

Put the white sauce in a heavy based saucepan over a high heat and slowly bring to the boil. Stir in the port, stirring slowly.

Take the pan off the heat and blend in the Stilton, meat glaze and mushrooms. Return the pan to the heat and add the mushroom ketchup and butter, melting it in by moving the saucepan in a circular motion until the butter is completely absorbed. Taste and adjust the seasoning. Sprinkle with the mint and parsley.

France

Duckling with Breton Cider Sauce

Once a year my family pays homage to the place that I consider to be one of the most important areas of France, Brittany. One day I hope to retire there, in the peace and tranquillity of Erquay, were time does not matter and the pace of life is very relaxed and has its own distinctive culture.

The Bretons are great lovers of duckling, so it's not surprising that when they cook it in the local cider the result is superb. Mireille Johnston is one of France's leading cooks with strong opinions about the food and produce of France, and she agrees with me that colour, fragrance and natural flavours are the essence of the Bretons' food. *Makes about 450ml/ 15fl oz.*

2.75kg/6 lb duckling, ready for roasting
600ml/1 pint dry Breton cider
225g/8oz shallots, chopped
100g/4oz rindless streaky bacon, diced
2 sprigs of dry thyme
2 sprigs of dry tarragon
225ml/8fl oz demi-glace sauce (page 35)
150ml/5fl oz fromage frais
100g/4oz mushrooms, sliced
2 apples, peeled, cored and sliced
40g/1½oz wild cherries
salt and freshly milled black pepper

Marinate the duckling for one day with the cider, shallots, bacon, thyme, tarragon and salt and pepper.

The next day, preheat the oven to 190°C/ 375°F/gas mark 5. Remove the duck from the marinade (reserve the marinade) and pat it dry, then roast it for 35 minutes. Set it aside until it is cool enough to handle. Pour the cooking juices into a saucepan and allow to cool so you can skim any excess fat from the surface.

Remove the duckling bones and slice the meat very thinly. Place the meat on a warmed serving platter in the turned-off oven.

Meanwhile, boil the cooking juices and reserved marinade until reduced by half. Add the demi-glace sauce and simmer for 10 minutes. Fold in the fromage frais and sliced mushrooms. Taste and adjust the seasoning.

Pour the sauce around the duck, garnish with slices of fresh apple and top with fresh wild cherries.

Sauce Gibier

Pheasant breasts cooked with juniper berries and served with this game sauce make a festive lunch. *Makes about 200ml/7fl oz.*

150ml/5fl oz port
150ml/5fl oz Madeira
150ml/5fl oz brandy
1 sprig of fresh thyme
1 sprig of fresh rosemary
grated rind of 1 orange
grated rind of 1 lemon
2 tablespoons red wine vinegar
1 teaspoon dried juniper berries
600ml/1 pint game stock (page 22)
25g/1oz best quality unsalted butter, diced
2 tablespoons double cream
salt and freshly milled black pepper

Put the port, Madeira, half the brandy, the thyme, rosemary, orange and lemon rinds, vinegar and juniper berries in a saucepan over a high heat and boil until the liquids reduce by two-thirds.

Add the game stock and continue boiling until the liquids reduce by a further one-third. Whisk in the butter, then stir in the remaining brandy and the cream.

Pass the sauce through a fine non-metallic sieve. Taste and adjust the seasoning.

Sauce Vierge

This olive oil and basil sauce must be served fresh, and it is excellent with grilled Dover sole. Peter Smith, at the Forge in Mattersey, near Doncaster, uses extra virgin oil and serves it with thin slices of salmon and turbot.

Some chefs include garlic in this recipe, I do not like it because I think it overpowers the other flavours. *Makes about 100ml/4fl oz.*

2 tomatoes
100ml/4fl oz olive oil
1 tablespoon lemon juice
1 teaspoon crushed coriander seeds
10 basil leaves, cut into thin strips
1 tablespoon chopped fresh parsley
salt and freshly milled white pepper

Plunge the tomatoes into a saucepan of boiling water for about 30 seconds, then place them under running cold water to refresh them and stop the cooking. Peel and seed the tomatoes and cut the flesh into small dice and place to one side.

Heat the olive oil in a small saucepan over a medium heat, stir in the lemon juice and remove the pan from the heat. Add the coriander, basil and parsley and leave the mixture to stand for at least 3 minutes.

Season, adding the diced tomato. Serve immediately with your favourite fish.

Truffle Sauces

Truffles are very expensive mushrooms, and the best are from the Périgord region of France. Because of their expense they were a rare and somewhat unusual ingredient not so long ago, but after the popularity of television shows such as *A Year in Provence* and *Chef*, they have become better known. If you can afford any, you will enjoy these wonderful sauces, but if your budget doesn't stretch to such luxury, I am afraid there is no substitute.

Truffle Sauce

Prepare a Madeira sauce (page 35) and add 1 whole truffle cut into 0.5cm/¼in dice to the hot sauce. Because truffles are so expensive, I suggest you serve this only with the best cuts, such as a fillet or tenderloin, of beef, pork, lamb and veal.

VARIATIONS

Sauce Périgueux Prepare as for the truffle sauce but add 1 tablespoon roughly chopped truffle to the Madeira sauce instead of diced truffle.

Sauce Rossini Prepare as for the truffle sauce but add 1 tablespoon sliced truffle instead of the diced truffle. For an even richer sauce, add 100g/4oz wild mushrooms that have been fried in a little butter and flamed with 1 tablespoon brandy.

Steak Rossini

Grill a fillet steak to your liking, then put the steak on a plate on top of a round of toast. Spread the top of the steak with smooth pâté and spoon over *sauce Rossini*.

To preserve fresh truffles

Scrub the truffles with vegetable brush and place them in a preserving jar and cover them completely with port. Seal the jar so it is air-tight and keep it in the fridge. The truffles will keep for at least 6 months this way.

Germany

Fresh Ox Tongue with Raisin Sauce

Not everything from Germany is hot bratswurst, sauerkraut and mustard, as this recipe illustrates. *Serves 4.*

1 cooked ox tongue, kept warm

for the raisin sauce
300ml / 10fl oz Bordelaise sauce (page 35)
75g / 3oz raisins
50g / 2oz currants
finely chopped rind of 1 lemon
1 tablespoon white wine vinegar
1 teaspoon brown sugar
1 tablespoon finely chopped almonds
1 tablespoon lemon juice
salt and freshly milled black pepper

Warm the Bordelaise sauce in a saucepan over a medium heat, then add the remaining ingredients, except the almonds and lemon juice, and simmer for 15 minutes, stirring occasionally.

Slice the tongue and arrange it on a warm serving platter. Add the almonds and lemon juice to the sauce and taste and adjust the seasoning. Pour the sauce around the tongue and serve.

VARIATION

German Game Sauce Add 2 tablespoons port jelly and 75g/3oz cooked cranberries to the raisin sauce along with the raisins and currants.

Greece

Egg and Lemon Sauce

Called *avgolemono*, this is traditionally served with lamb at Easter in Greece. In my research, I have found a 19th-century version of this recipe that replaces the egg with liver to make a lemon and liver sauce. Take care not to let this sauce boil or it will curdle. *Makes about 175ml/6fl oz.*

150ml/5fl oz meat velouté sauce (page 26)
1 teaspoon dried dill
3 eggs
freshly squeezed juice of 2 large lemons
salt and freshly milled black pepper

Place the velouté sauce in a saucepan over a medium heat, add the dried dill and let it stand for 4 minutes; it must not be boiling but remain hot.

Season the sauce with salt and pepper. Beat the eggs lightly in a bowl and stir in the lemon juice. Slowly add 4 tablespoons of the hot sauce, whisking all the time, then whisk in the remaining hot sauce slowly.

Return the sauce to the pan over a very low heat and cook for no more than 2 minutes to warm through, whisking constantly. Taste and adjust the seasoning.

Moussaka

I've devised this recipe so you can enjoy the flavour of eating at a Greek taverna. *Serves 4–6.*

3 large aubergines, sliced about 1cm / ½in thick
3 tablespoons cooking oil
1 large onion, sliced
2 garlic cloves, chopped
450g / 1lb minced lamb or vegetarian filling
2 tablespoons tomato purée
75ml/3fl oz red wine
1 teaspoon ground cinnamon
1 tablespoon chopped fresh parsley
salt and freshly milled black pepper

for the moussaka sauce
300ml / 10fl oz cheese sauce (pages 25–6)
25g / 1oz butter, softened and diced
1 tablespoon rose petal vinegar (page 16)
50g / 2oz Edam cheese, grated
freshly grated nutmeg

Place the aubergines in a colander and sprinkle with salt, cover, press them down and leave them to drain for 35 minutes. Rinse them well with cold water and pat dry.

Heat 2 tablespoons oil in a large saucepan over a medium heat, add the onion and garlic and fry for a few minutes, then stir in the lamb or vegetarian filling, tomato purée, red wine, cinnamon, parsley and salt and pepper. Stir until well blended, then lower the heat and simmer for 25 minutes.

Heat a little more oil in a frying pan and fry the aubergines on both sides until golden brown, working in batches if necessary. Place them on absorbent kitchen towels to drain.

To make the sauce, heat the cheese sauce in a saucepan over a low heat, slowly add little pieces of butter and stirring all the time. Add the vinegar and cheese and continue simmering for 2 minutes. Season with freshly grated nutmeg, salt and pepper.

Preheat the oven to 180°C/350°F/gas mark 4. Layer the lamb or vegetarian filling, aubergine slices and sauce in an ovenproof dish, ending with a layer of sauce that covers the top. Bake for about 45 minutes.

Skorthalia

Here are two versions of this classic Greek garlic sauce. The first, made with a fish velouté sauce, I serve in the winter with fish dishes and vegetables. The second version is made with wine vinegar and olive oil, and I serve it chilled or at room temperature during the summer months with salmon. Cypriots always serve this with wedges of lemon for squeezing over and juicy black olives. *Each recipe makes about 300ml/10fl oz.*

Method 1
300ml/10fl oz fish velouté sauce (page 26)
4 garlic cloves, crushed
50g/2oz ground almonds
50g/2oz extra-fine fresh brown breadcrumbs
lemon juice, to taste
salt and freshly milled black pepper

Place the velouté sauce, garlic, ground almonds and breadcrumbs in a saucepan and simmer for 20 minutes. Pass through a fine sieve, then add a few drops of lemon juice. Taste and adjust the seasoning.

Method 2
150g/5oz fresh white breadcrumbs
300ml/10fl oz fish stock (pages 19–20)
4 garlic cloves
50g/2oz ground almonds
2 tablespoons chopped fresh parsley
1 tablespoon white wine vinegar
5 tablespoons virgin olive oil
50g/2oz ground almonds
salt and freshly milled black pepper

Soak the breadcrumbs in a little fish stock for 10 minutes, then squeeze out the moisture. But the breadcrumbs in a bowl and stir in the garlic, almonds and parsley. Whisk in the wine vinegar, then slowly whisk in the olive oil. Taste and adjust the seasoning.

Hungary

Veal Cutlets with Paprika Sauce

Among the most famous of all Hungarian recipes are the *gulyás* and the *paprikás*. This is a simple *papriká* recipe, which is served in most Hungarian households every week, usually with boiled sauerkraut and Hussar toast (*huszar-rostelyos*). When you are ready to serve, put the sliced apple on a warm serving dish, put the bacon rashers on top, then place the veal cutlets around the dish and pour the sauce over them. Sprinkle with fresh parsley.

To make the toast, fry 4 pieces of stale bread in goose fat until golden brown, sprinkle with salt and rub the bread with freshly crushed garlic. *Serves 4.*

25g / 1oz butter
8 rindless back bacon rashers
4 × 225g / 8oz veal cutlets, trimmed

150ml/5fl oz veal stock (page 21)
1 tablespoon paprika
300ml/10fl oz sour cream
1 apple, cored and sliced
1 tablespoon finely chopped fresh parsley
salt and freshly milled black pepper

Melt the butter in a frying pan over a medium heat. Add the bacon rashers and fry until they are crispy. Remove them from the pan and keep warm.

Add the veal cutlets to the pan and fry them in the bacon fat and butter until they are a golden brown colour. Stir in the veal stock and simmer until the cutlets are quite tender. Season with salt and the paprika. Add the sour cream and stir until the sauce thickens.

India

Beef Korma

The historian in me cannot resist sharing with you this recipe from 1865, which I have converted for 20th-century tastes.

The *dahi* used in this recipe is a curd cheese made by adding a little vinegar or tartaric acid to boiled milk while it is still warm and then leaving it to set for 12 hours.

During that time the mixture thickens until it is like a very thick cream. In India, *dahi* is also eaten with salt and rice or served with sugar as a sweet. Natural yogurt and sour cream are good substitutes for *dahi. Serves 4.*

50g/2oz butter
2 tablespoons minced shallots
3 onions, sliced
3 garlic cloves
1 teaspoon coriander seed
1 teaspoon ground chillies
1 teaspoon each of turmeric and ground ginger
6 ground cardamom seeds
2 cloves
2 sticks cinnamon, finely ground
pinch of saffron
450g/1 lb rump steak, trimmed and cubed
150ml/5fl oz meat stock (pages 20–21)
225g/8oz dahi (see above)
100ml/4fl oz lemon juice
salt and freshly milled black pepper

Preheat the oven to 180°C/350°F/gas mark 4. Melt the butter in a large flameproof casserole over a medium heat, then add the shallots and onions and fry until they are brown, stirring frequently. Stir in the garlic and all the spices until they are well blended, then continue cooking for 3 minutes, stirring frequently.

Add the beef and cook for about 5 minutes until it browns on all sides.

Pour in the beef stock, cover the casserole and cook for 1 hour until the beef is almost tender.

Remove the casserole from the oven and fold in the *dahi* or sour cream and lemon juice. Return the casserole to the oven and continue cooking for a further 15 minutes. Taste and adjust the seasoning.

Ireland

Beef with Guinness Sauce

One of the most beautiful areas in Ireland is without doubt Bray in Co. Wicklow, home of Woodbrook Golf Club . . . and this traditional Irish recipe. I serve it with boiled cabbage and new potatoes. *Serves 6.*

3 tablespoons cooking oil
450g / 1lb sirloin steak, any fat and gristle
   removed and cubed
100g / 4oz rindless streaky back bacon, diced and
   fried crispy
100g / 4oz button mushrooms, sliced
100g / 4oz baby onions, halved
1 onion, sliced
1 garlic clove, crushed
3 tablespoons red wine vinegar
300ml / 10fl oz draught Guinness
300ml / 10fl oz perfect gravy (pages 44–5), or
   other leftover gravy

Heat the oil in a large saucepan over a high heat, add the steak, bacon, mushrooms, onions and garlic and fry for 8 minutes, stirring frequently, until the steak cubes are browned on all sides. Stir in the red wine vinegar and continue frying for 2 minutes.

Pour in the Guinness and let the mixture simmer for 12 minutes. Add the gravy and continue to simmer for 12 minutes.

A Very Good Irish Sauce

I've adapted this recipe from a 19th-century manuscript, and I think it is particularly good when served with hake, lemon sole or herring. *Makes about 225ml/8fl oz.*

150ml / 5fl oz perfect gravy (pages 44–5), or
   other leftover gravy
8 anchovy fillets, finely chopped
2 tablespoons white wine vinegar
1 teaspoon grated fresh horseradish
pinch each of ground mace and grated nutmeg
pinch fresh sweet marjoram
pinch finely chopped fresh parsley
2 cloves
6 black peppercorns
2 shallots, finely chopped
1 tablespoon tomato purée
25g / 1oz butter, melted

Put the gravy in a saucepan and slowly bring to the boil, then lower the heat to very low and simmer for 6 minutes.

Add the anchovy fillets and all the remaining ingredients, except the butter, and continue simmering until the sauce is reduced by half.

Pass the sauce through a fine non-metallic sieve and stir in the butter.

Pears in a Wild Mint Vinaigrette

This Irish recipe is from one of the oldest hotels in Bray, the Royal. The combination of this with cold roast pork and a bottle of chilled dry white wine is my idea of luxury. *Serves 4–6.*

1 head of crisp lettuce, separated into leaves and rinsed
4 ripe dessert pears, peeled, cored and sliced

for the vinaigrette
6 tablespoons olive oil
3 tablespoons white wine vinegar
2 tablespoons finely chopped fresh wild mint
1 tablespoon clear honey
1 tablespoon Dijon mustard
1 teaspoon ground cloves
2 tablespoons finely chopped fresh parsley
salt and freshly ground white pepper

Place all the vinaigrette ingredients in a large bowl. Add the sliced pears and gently spoon the dressing over them, cover and chill for at least 2 hours.

Meanwhile, place the lettuce leaves around the sides of a serving platter and place in the refrigerator.

When you are ready to serve, arrange the pears on the lettuce leaves and sprinkle with a little of the vinaigrette.

Italy

Bolognese Sauce

I've had a very long discussion with London restaurateur Antonio Carluccio, whose great passion is pasta, about the relationship of pasta dishes and sauces. We have promised to get together to create interesting recipes using both, and I'm really looking forward to that event. But in the meanwhile, try this Italian recipe created by a Lancashire lad . . .

If you like only the best, this is the recipe for you. I promise you it is the best Bolognese sauce you will ever taste. Serve it with home-made pasta and freshly grated Parmesan cheese. I haven't included any garlic in the ingredients but feel free to add as much as you like. *Makes about 450g/1lb.*

25g/1oz best-quality butter
2 tablespoons virgin olive oil
8 shallots, finely chopped
1 carrot, cut into small pieces
1 celery stick, finely chopped
2 bay leaves
450g/1lb coarsely minced fillet of beef
150ml/5fl oz Marsala
100g/4oz button mushrooms, sliced
20g/¾oz tomato purée
150ml/5fl oz veal stock (page 21)
salt and freshly ground black pepper

Melt the butter with the olive oil in a large saucepan over a medium heat. Add the shallots, carrot, celery and bay leaves and fry, stirring often, until the vegetables soften.

Add the beef and mix together, then continue cooking for a further 5 minutes, stirring constantly. Pour in the Marsala and continue simmering until it has completely evaporated.

Add the mushrooms, tomato purée and stock and bring to the boil, then lower the heat and simmer for 15 minutes until the stock is reduced by half. Taste and adjust the seasoning.

Genovese Sauce for Fish

Serve this with freshly grilled trout, mullet or salmon. *Makes about 175ml/6fl oz.*

1 tablespoon capers, well drained
2 anchovy fillets, chopped
3 stuffed olives, chopped
yolk of 1 hard-boiled egg
1 tablespoon fresh breadcrumbs soaked in
2 tablespoons wine vinegar
1 tablespoon chopped fresh parsley
1 garlic clove, crushed
150ml/5fl oz olive oil
1 tablespoon white wine vinegar
3 tablespoons lemon juice
salt and freshly milled black pepper

Pound together the capers, anchovies, olives, egg yolk, soaked breadcrumbs, parsley and garlic in a bowl until the mixture resembles a very smooth paste. Slowly beat in the olive oil, then add the vinegar. Taste and adjust the seasoning, then add the lemon juice. Taste again.

Sauce Italienne

You could argue that this sauce, and the variations, are actually French recipes, but the spirit of the recipe is surely Italian, so I've included them here. For a perfect evening with your loved one, candles and light music, put 450g/ 1lb freshly cubed fillet of lamb in a casserole, sprinkle with tarragon and pour over this sauce. Bake for 40 minutes in an oven pre-heated to 180°C/350°F/gas mark 4, then serve with home-made pasta and a glass of good Italian wine. *The sauce makes about 300ml/ 10fl oz.*

    25g/1oz butter
    1 tablespoon olive oil
    25g/1oz shallots, chopped
    1 garlic clove, crushed
    50g/2oz button mushrooms, chopped
    25g/1oz boneless veal shank, minced
    25g/1oz minced beef
    1 tablespoon wine vinegar
    1 clove
    pinch of fresh thyme
    300ml/10fl oz pepper sauce (pages 37–8)
    100g/4oz tomatoes, seeded and diced
    3 tablespoons tomato purée
    1 sprig of fresh tarragon
    salt and freshly milled black pepper

Melt the butter with the olive oil in a large frying pan, then add the shallots and garlic and fry gently for 2 minutes until the shallots are softened. Add the mushrooms, veal and beef, season to your taste and continue cooking for 6 minutes over a medium heat, stirring occasionally. Add the wine vinegar, clove and thyme and continue cooking for a further 2 minutes. Stir in the pepper sauce and simmer for at least 20 minutes until the sauce reduces slightly.

Stir in the tomatoes, tomato purée and tarragon and continue simmering for a further 15 minutes. Taste and adjust the seasoning.

VARIATIONS

Bulgare Sauce Fry 75g/3oz diced celery with the shallots. Serve this with beef.

Byron Sauce Add 150ml/5fl oz claret and boil to reduce, then add some chopped truffles. Serve with game and pork dishes.

Sauce Czardas Season with 1 tablespoon paprika and stir in 150ml/5fl oz double cream when the sauce has finished simmering. Serve with roast beef and veal.

Sauce Françoise Add 75g/3oz sliced mushrooms and fry them with the shallots, then stir in 25g/1oz softened butter at the end to enrich the sauce. Serve this with veal, seafood and chicken.

Tomato and Beef Sauce Replace the veal with ground beef.

Marsala Sauce

I could not consider a section on Italian sauces without including this sauce made from Marsala, the best known Sicilian wine. This sauce, traditionally served with fillet of beef, was created by John Woodhouse, an Englishman who started to produce wine at Marsala in 1773. *Makes about 300ml/10fl oz.*

600ml/1 pint Espagnole sauce (pages 38–9)
150ml/5fl oz Marsala

Put the Espagnole sauce in a saucepan over a high heat and boil until it is reduced by half. In a separate pan, boil the Marsala until it is reduced by one-third, then stir the two ingredients together.

VARIATION
Sauce Colbert Add 3 tablespoons Marsala, 1 teaspoon finely chopped fresh parsley and 2 tablespoons lemon juice to the reduced Espagnole sauce, then whisk in 25g/1oz softened butter at the end to enrich the sauce. Serve with fried fish.

Pesto Sauce

Here's a classic Italian sauce that's unbeatable with home-made pasta. Place 2 garlic cloves, 50g/2oz pine nuts or walnuts, 50g/2oz fresh basil leaves and 50g/2oz freshly grated Parmesan cheese in a blender of food processor and blend together. Add 150ml/5fl oz olive oil with a generous pinch of salt. *Makes about 175ml/6fl oz.*

Tomato Sauce

The finest tomato sauce I have ever had! This 'international' sauce could just as easily be classified as Spanish, but it really does make the most of ripe Italian tomatoes, so I've included it in this section. I was given this recipe by friends in Palma who said you must always use Spanish onions, but Italian tomatoes and the finest virgin olive oil with a touch of England (Worcestershire sauce) are just as good. *Makes about 200ml/7fl oz.*

25g/1oz butter
4 tablespoons virgin olive oil
1 Spanish onion, finely chopped
2 garlic cloves, crushed
800g/1¾ lb Italian tomatoes, skinned and finely chopped
6 tablespoons dry red wine
1 bay leaf
pinch each of dried oregano and ground cumin
100ml/4fl oz pepper sauce (pages 37 8)
6 tablespoons tomato purée
1 tablespoon Worcestershire sauce
salt and freshly milled black pepper

Melt the butter with the olive oil in a large frying pan over a medium heat, then add the onion and garlic and fry until the onion is soft and transparent, stirring frequently.

Add the tomatoes, wine and bay leaf, oregano and cumin and boil until the mixture is reduced by half, then add the pepper sauce and tomato purée and continue boiling for a further 10 minutes. Season well, lower the heat and leave the sauce to simmer for 15 minutes.

Pass the sauce through a fine sieve. Stir in the Worcestershire sauce just before serving. Taste and adjust the seasoning.

Japan

Prawns with Peanut Sauce

This makes a very good starter or light lunch, and you can also serve the sauce with other shellfish or seafood. Lobster tails make a spectacular garnish if your budget can run to it, but otherwise lemon and lime slices are just as impressive. *Makes about 250ml/9fl oz.*

2 tablespoons peanut oil
1 garlic, chopped
100g / 4oz salted peanuts
1 fresh red chilli, seeded and finely chopped
1 teaspoon grated fresh root ginger
pinch of ground cinnamon
75g / 3oz raw tiger prawns, unshelled
3 tablespoons saké
300ml / 10fl oz fish stock (pages 19–20)
1 tablespoon honey
juice of 1 lime
finely grated rind and juice of 1 lemon
1 tablespoon blond roux (page 23)
salt and freshly milled white pepper
lemon and lime slices, to garnish

Heat the peanut oil in a saucepan over a medium heat, add the garlic, peanuts, chilli, ginger, cinnamon, prawns and saké and cook for 3 minutes, stirring all the time. Slowly add the fish stock and remove the tiger prawns as soon as they turn pink. Take care not to let the sauce boil, or the prawns will become tough.

Stir in the honey, lime juice, lemon rind and juice, the roux and salt and pepper, then leave the sauce to simmer for 30 minutes over a low heat.

Peel the prawns and pass the sauce through a fine sieve. Return the prawns to the sauce just long enough to heat through but do not boil. Serve the prawns in the sauce with a lemon and lime garnish.

New Zealand

Lamb Fillet with Kiwi Sauce

At the beginning of the 1990s we had kiwi fruit coming out of our ears, after a mad advertising campaign from New Zealand introduced the odd-looking fruit to Europe. Yet, New Zealanders did not have a traditional sauce using kiwi fruit, so I developed this one to go with their delicious lamb. *Serves 4.*

150ml / 5fl oz meat stock (pages 20–21)
1 garlic clove, crushed
1 teaspoon dried mint
1 teaspoon fresh basil
1 teaspoon red wine vinegar
8 kiwi fruit, peeled and diced
good pinch of cayenne pepper
450g / 1lb neck fillet of lamb
150ml / 5fl oz Espagnole sauce (pages 38–9),
    warm
25g / 1oz softened butter mixed with 25g / 1oz
    plain flour
4 kiwi fruit, peeled and thinly sliced
fresh sprig each of mint and basil, to garnish

Place the meat stock, garlic, mint, basil, vinegar, kiwi fruit and cayenne pepper in a saucepan over a high heat and bring to the boil. Lower the heat and simmer until the stock reduces by half. Press the mixture through a fine sieve into a clean saucepan, then set aside.

Meanwhile, preheat the oven to 220°C/425°F/gas mark 7.

Place the lamb fillet in an ovenproof dish and pour over the Espagnole sauce. Place in the oven for 25 minutes, then remove the fillets from the dish and keep them warm in the turned-off oven.

Transfer the cooking juices to the kiwi and stock mixture and bring to the boil, then lower the heat and simmer for 15 minutes. Stir in the butter and flour mixture and allow the sauce to simmer for 15 minutes to thicken. Serve the lamb fillets garnished with the sliced kiwi fruit and fresh herb sprigs.

Lime Sauce

Serve this refreshing sauce with lamb cutlets or sliced leg of lamb. *Makes about 350ml/12fl oz.*

300ml / 10fl oz meat stock (pages 20–21)
4 shallots, sliced
1 teaspoon grated fresh root ginger
1 teaspoon crushed rosemary
finely grated rind and juice of 2 limes
2 tablespoons honey
2 tablespoons red wine vinegar
150ml / 5fl oz velouté sauce (page 26)
salt and freshly milled white pepper

Place all the ingredients, except the velouté sauce, in a saucepan over a high heat and bring to the boil, then lower the heat and simmer until the sauce is reduced by half.

Stir in the velouté sauce and simmer until reduced by half again. Taste and adjust the seasoning.

Portugal

Lemon and Tarragon Sauce

This sauce is excellent served with chicken. *Makes about 300ml/10fl oz.*

> 300ml/10fl oz béchamel sauce (page 26)
> 150ml/5fl oz milk
> 2 tablespoons double cream
> juice and thinly sliced rind of 2 lemons
> 1 tablespoon dried tarragon
> 1 tablespoon tarragon vinegar
> salt and freshly milled white pepper
> 1 sprig of fresh tarragon, to garnish

Put the béchamel sauce in a saucepan and keep warm. In a separate pan, combine the milk, cream, lemon rind and juice, dried tarragon and vinegar. Bring to the boil, then lower the heat as low as possible and leave the ingredients to infuse for at least 5 minutes.

Slowly pour the infused liquid through a fine non-metallic sieve into the béchamel sauce. Allow the sauce to simmer for 5 minutes, then taste and adjust the seasoning. Serve garnished with a sprig of tarragon.

Loin of Veal, Portuguese Style

Working in Portugal in the 1970s was not my idea of a good time: the sun was very hot, the political uprising had just started and I had to drive there three times a year from England, passing through France and Spain to arrive in Lisbon eight days later. There were a few good things that came out of my time in Portugal, however, such as my favourite vintage port and Madeira and this dish. *Serves 4–6.*

> 2 kg/4½ lb loin of veal, boned
> 1 bottle Madeira
> 8 shallots, sliced
> 3 garlic cloves
> 300ml/10fl oz demi-glace sauce (page 35) or veal stock (page 21)
> salt and freshly milled black pepper

The day before you plan to serve this, place the veal in a deep non-metallic casserole with the Madeira, shallots and garlic and season well. Let the veal stand for 24 hours at room temperature in the marinade, turning it every 2 hours when possible.

The next day, preheat the oven to 180°C/350°F/gas mark 4. Remove half the Madeira from the casserole and reserve. Place the casserole in the oven for 1½ hours, basting frequently. Turn up the heat to 220°C/425°F/gas mark 7 for the last 15 minutes.

Meanwhile, place the reserved Madeira in a saucepan over a high heat and boil until it is reduced by two-thirds. Add the demi-glace sauce and simmer for a further 5 minutes. Taste and adjust the seasoning.

Remove the veal from the casserole and leave it to stand for at least 5 minutes. Slice the meat and place it on to a warm serving dish with the sauce in a sauce boat.

Olive Sauce

Try this with your favourite meat or poultry for a taste of the Algarve. *Makes about 300ml/10fl oz.*

300ml/10fl oz Espagnole sauce (pages 38–9)
150ml/5fl oz chicken stock (page 21)
24 small stoned olives, sliced
1 tablespoon lemon juice
1 tablespoon chopped fresh parsley
salt and freshly milled black pepper

Heat the Espagnole sauce in a saucepan over a medium heat. Put the chicken stock, olives, lemon juice and parsley in another pan and bring to the boil, then simmer for 20 minutes. Stir in the Espagnole sauce and continue simmering for a further 30 minutes. Taste and adjust the seasoning.

Salsa Pizzaiola

I recommend that you pour this sauce over root vegetables in an ovenproof dish and bake them until they are tender. Serve the vegetables with jacket potatoes with sour cream for a delicious vegetarian meal. *Makes about 200ml/7fl oz.*

3 tablespoons olive oil
8 shallots, finely chopped
3 garlic cloves, crushed
450g/1 lb tomatoes, chopped
2 tablespoons tomato purée
1 tablespoon fresh oregano leaves
1 teaspoon chopped fresh basil
1 tablespoon sugar
salt and freshly milled white pepper

Heat the oil in a saucepan over a medium heat, add the shallots and garlic and fry for 2 minutes, stirring occasionally.

Add the remaining ingredients and bring to the boil, then lower the heat and simmer for 30 minutes over a very low heat. Taste and adjust the seasoning.

Sauce for Loin of Pork

I relax by playing golf (not very well, I might add), and the Algarve is where I like to play the game, and also eat. Portugal is a pleasure dome for foodies, as the country has a wealth of traditional sauces (*molhos*) to appreciate. A succulent roasted loin of pork served with this sauce is one of the dishes I always look forward to during my visits. *Serves 4.*

2 tablespoons olive oil
3 garlic cloves, crushed
6 shallots, sliced
75g/3oz mushrooms, sliced
1 sprig of fresh thyme
150ml/5fl oz dry white wine, such as
   Chardonnay
1 tablespoon lemon juice
1 tablespoon tomato purée
150ml/5fl oz Espagnole sauce (pages 38–9)
salt and freshly milled black pepper

Heat the olive oil in a flameproof casserole over a medium heat, add the garlic, shallots and mushrooms and fry for 2 minutes, stirring occasionally. Add the thyme and continue frying for a further 2 minutes.

Stir in the white wine and lemon juice and boil until the liquids are reduce by half. Remove the thyme and stir in the tomato purée. Slowly stir in the Espagnole sauce and salt and pepper, then simmer for 12 minutes. Taste and adjust the seasoning.

Scandinavia

Danish Blue Cheese Sauce

The Scandinavian countries of Denmark, Finland, Iceland, Norway and Sweden have one thing in common – fish, fish and more fish, invariably served with gravlax and gallons of sour cream! To introduce some variety, I devised this interesting recipe. And fish need not be the only food this sauce can be served with – try cubes of bread, asparagus, broccoli, celery, melon and cucumber, interspersed with cubes of cooked ham and apple. Pork and freshly cooked prawns can be dipped into the sauce to make an interesting fondue. It is also excellent served with roast fillet of pork and freshly baked apples. *Makes about 300ml/ 10fl oz.*

    100g / 4oz Danish blue cheese, softened and
        crumbled
    1 teaspoon white wine vinegar
    1 tablespoon apple purée
    1 teaspoon mild mustard
    2 egg yolks
    300ml / 10fl oz velouté sauce (page 26), warmed
    few drops lemon juice
    25g / 1oz unsalted butter (optional)
    salt and freshly milled white pepper

Blend the cheese, vinegar, apple purée and mustard together in a bowl with the egg yolks. Slowly whisk in the warm velouté sauce. Place the sauce mixture in a saucepan and bring gently just to boiling point, then simmer over a very low heat, gently whisking, until the sauce thickens.

Add the lemon juice and salt and pepper. Whisk in the butter just before serving to give the sauce a glaze, if you want.

Dill Sas

This traditional Swedish sauce is made by blending 1 tablespoon hot clarified butter with 2 tablespoons plain flour in a saucepan over a medium heat and stirring frequently for about 3 minutes. Gradually stir in 600ml/1 pint fish stock (pages 19–20) and 2 tablespoons fresh dill, 1 tablespoon wine vinegar, 2 teaspoons sugar and salt and freshly milled black pepper. Whisk together thoroughly, then whisk in 1 egg yolk.

Spain

Green Sauce

Traditionally this is served with mussels, but it goes well with most seafood. *Makes about 300ml/10fl oz.*

4 tablespoons olive oil
3 garlic cloves, chopped
50g / 2oz plain flour
600ml / 1 pint meat stock (pages 20–21), hot
2 tablespoons chopped fresh parsley
2 tablespoons chopped cooked spinach
50g / 2oz cooked peas
50g / 2oz asparagus tips, chopped
salt and freshly milled black pepper

Heat the olive oil in a saucepan over medium heat, then add the garlic and fry until it begins to turn brown. Stir in flour and gradually add the stock, parsley and spinach. Season well and leave to simmer until the sauce reduces by one-third.

Add the peas and asparagus tips and continue simmering for 10 minutes. Taste and adjust the seasoning.

VARIATIONS

Canary Island Red Sauce Omit the green vegetables and add 1 teaspoon paprika and 1 teaspoon crushed dried chilli. Serve this with seafood.

Pine Nut Sauce Omit the paprika and dried chilli in the Canary Island red sauce (above); instead, add 200g/7oz crushed pine nuts and cook them for 5 minutes. Serve this with chicken or veal.

Olive Sauce Omit the pine nuts from the pine nut sauce (above) and instead add 150g/5oz stoned green olives, 2 peeled, seeded and chopped tomatoes and 4 tablespoons dry sherry. Serve this with fish and game.

Thailand

Pork Curry

Thai curries are milder and creamier than those made in India or in the Caribbean, and the sauces usually contain coconut milk, such as this one. *Serves 4.*

2 tablespoons peanut oil
225g / 8oz pork tenderloin, diced
1 small aubergine, diced
2 garlic cloves, crushed
1 red pepper, seeded and thinly sliced
1 teaspoon mild curry paste
150ml / 5fl oz tinned creamed coconut milk
2 tablespoons soy sauce
1 tablespoon oyster sauce (page 61)
1 teaspoon cornflour blended with a little coconut milk
finely chopped fresh parsley
1 tablespoon thick double cream
salt and freshly milled black pepper

Heat the peanut oil in a large saucepan over a medium heat, add the pork, aubergine and garlic and cook slowly for 8 minutes, stirring all the time.

Add all the pepper, curry paste, coconut milk and soy and oyster sauces and continue simmering for a further 5 minutes. Stir in the cornflour mixture and continue simmering until the sauce thickens slightly.

Finally add the parsley and double cream. Taste and adjust the seasoning. Serve on to a plate of fried wild rice.

Fondue Sauces

Fondue Bourguignonne

This recipe is very expensive, but I guarantee your fondue will be talked about for years to come. To make this recipe perfect, use a double boiler or a copper saucepan. *Makes about 700ml/24fl oz.*

6 egg yolks
150ml/5fl oz water
150ml/5fl oz rose petal vinegar (page 16)
600ml/1 pint virgin olive oil, warmed
2 tablespoons Dijon mustard
2 tablespoons tomato purée
2 tablespoons anchovy purée or crushed
  anchovies
1 tablespoon thinly sliced truffle strips
salt and freshly milled white pepper

Blend the eggs yolks, water and vinegar together in a bowl. Place them in a copper pan over a very low heat, or in the top of a double boiler, or in a heatproof bowl over a pan of simmering water. Whisk until the mixture becomes frothy and quite firm. Season with salt and pepper.

Whisk in the oil a little at a time, adding it very slowly until it is all absorbed. Place the mustard, tomato purée and anchovy purée or anchovies into separate clear bowls. Divide the sauce equally between the bowls and blend together.

Sprinkle the truffle over each bowl.

Place the dishes on one large platter and surround them with your favourite hot vegetables, cubes of French bread and cooked cubes of meat or fish, ready to dip into the fondue.

Gruyère Sauce

This is excellent for using in a fondue with finger-size pieces of lightly blanched courgettes, celery, cucumber and broccoli and cauliflower florets. *Makes about 400ml/14fl oz.*

300ml/10fl oz cheese sauce (pages 25–6)
100g/4oz Gruyère cheese, grated
pinch of grated nutmeg
1 tablespoon white wine vinegar
25g/1oz butter, softened

Gently heat the cheese sauce in a saucepan over a low heat, then stir in the cheese, nutmeg and vinegar. Simmer over a very low heat for 5 minutes, stirring. Just before serving, stir in little pieces of the softened butter.

Luxury Swiss Fondue Sauce

This recipe from Neuchâtel could be called the Swiss national dish. The only cheeses to use are Emmenthal and Gruyère from Switzerland.

For a fondue party, serve with sticks of French bread, cut into bite-size cubes, a selection of lightly blanched fresh vegetables and fruit, cooked and shelled prawns and cubes of cooked ham with pineapple. *Makes about 400ml/14fl oz.*

1 garlic clove, halved
300ml / 10fl oz dry white wine
1 teaspoon white wine vinegar
200g / 7oz Emmenthal cheese, coarsely grated
400g / 14oz Gruyère cheese, coarsely grated
2 teaspoons cornflour
100ml / 4fl oz kirsch
freshly grated nutmeg
freshly milled black pepper

Rub the clove of garlic around the inside of an enamelled cast-iron or earthenware fondue pan. Heat the wine gently in a saucepan, then pour it into the fondue pan and stir in the wine vinegar. Put the fondue pan over the heat source.

Gradually add the cheeses, stirring the ingredients together. Slowly bring the sauce to the boil over the heat source, stirring constantly until the cheeses melt.

Blend the cornflour and kirsch together and stir into the cheese mixture. Add a pinch of nutmeg and pepper and the sauce is ready to use. Keep over a heat source while everyone dips in the bread, vegetables, fruit, prawns and ham and pineapple. If the sauce gets too thick, stir in a little milk.

Other Sauces for Using in a Fondue

- Use *beurre blanc* (page 29), adding your favourite herb and liquor to give the fondue party a boost.
- Bulgare Sauce (page 86)
- Byron Sauce (page 86)
- Sauce Czardas (page 86)
- Sauce Françoise (page 86)

Dressings and Dips

Make up your own dip recipes. Just blend three or four of your favourite herbs with lemon juice, yogurt, fromage frais or crème fraîche. If you like stronger flavours, stir in crushed garlic, a finely chopped chilli, Tabasco sauce or any hot spice.

French Dressing

Makes about 225ml/8fl oz.

175ml/6fl oz olive oil
4 tablespoons wine vinegar
2 teaspoons Dijon mustard
1 garlic clove, crushed
salt and freshly milled black pepper

Put all the ingredients into a bowl and whisk. Chill and whisk again before serving.

Honey and Lemon Dressing

Makes about 225ml/8fl oz.

finely grated rind and juice of 2 lemons
2 tablespoons clear honey
175ml/6fl oz olive oil
salt and freshly milled black pepper

Place all the ingredients into a bowl and whisk. Chill and whisk again before serving.

VARIATIONS

Tomato and Garlic Dressing Make a tomato, honey and lemon dressing (below) but replace the honey with 2 crushed garlic cloves.

Tomato, Honey and Lemon Dressing Add 150ml/5fl oz thick tomato juice and 2 tablespoons snipped fresh chives.

Guacamole Dip

Don't keep this for more than 2 days in the fridge, or it will start to turn brown. Serve with vegetable sticks or spicy corn chips. *Makes 150–200g/ 5–7 oz.*

2 avocados
juice of 1 lemon
2 garlic cloves, crushed
50g/2oz onion, grated
2 beef tomatoes, skinned, seeded and finely chopped
½ teaspoon chilli powder
Tabasco sauce
salt and freshly milled black pepper

Remove the flesh from the avocado and chop it up. Place it in a mixing bowl and spoon over the lemon juice.

Add the garlic, onion, tomatoes and chilli powder, Tabasco sauce and salt and pepper, blending thoroughly. A few drops of Tabasco are all that is required unless you want a really hot and spicy sauce, in which case add more chilli and Tabasco. Cover the bowl with cling film and refrigerate until required.

Sour Cream and Dill Dip

Serve this with bite-size vegetables, tacos, thick-cut crisps, cooked shellfish and crisp pieces fruit. I particularly like cucumber and celery matchsticks with this creamy dip. *Makes about 150ml/5fl oz.*

150ml/5fl oz sour cream
1 tablespoon chopped fresh dill
1 tablespoon lemon juice
salt and freshly milled black pepper

Blend all the ingredients together. Cover and chill until required.

Dessert Sauces

Quick Sweet White Sauce

This sauce will keep for up to two days in the fridge to be re-heated when it is required. *Makes about 300ml/10fl oz.*

300ml / 10fl oz milk
2 tablespoons caster sugar
a few drops of vanilla essence, or 2 tablespoons of your favourite tipple, such as whisky, rum or brandy
2 tablespoons cornflour blended with 2 tablespoons cold milk

Put the milk in a saucepan over a medium heat and slowly bring it to the boil. Add the sugar and vanilla or spirit and stir until the sugar dissolves, then lower the heat and simmer for 3 minutes, stirring frequently. Add the cornflour paste and continue simmering for 2 minutes.

VARIATIONS

Quick Sweet Almond Sauce Use the ingredients as above, but add 2 tablespoons ground almonds when adding the cornflour paste. Just before serving, stir in 4 drops almond essence.

Quick Sweet Chocolate Sauce Use the ingredients as above, but dissolve 2 tablespoons cocoa powder in the hot milk.

Quick Sweet Coffee Sauce Use the ingredients as above, but dissolve 2 tablespoons instant coffee in the hot milk.

Quick Sweet Ginger Sauce Use the ingredients as above, but add 1 tablespoon ground ginger to the cornflour when blending it with the cold milk.

Quick Sweet Liqueur Sauce Use the ingredients as above, but add 2 tablespoons of your favourite liqueur just before serving.

Quick Sweet Rum and Raisin Sauce Use the ingredients as above, but blend 1 tablespoon cocoa powder with the cornflour and substitute 2 tablespoons rum for the cold milk. When the sauce has finished simmering the first time, add 50g/2oz seedless raisins and continue simmering for a further 2 minutes.

Quick Chocolate Sauce

Serve this with a hot soufflé. *Makes about 300ml/10fl oz.*

175g/6oz best-quality dark chocolate, broken into small pieces
150ml/5fl oz single milk or top of milk
3 tablespoons sweet sherry

Combine the chocolate and milk in the top of a double boiler over a medium heat, or in a heatproof bowl set over a saucepan of simmering water. Stir until the chocolate melts, then whisk in the sherry.

Luxury Chocolate Sauce

This is delicious served hot with home-made ice cream. *Makes about 450ml/15fl oz.*

75g/3oz sugar
4 tablespoons water
100g/4oz Swiss dark chocolate, broken into pieces
2 egg yolks, size 3, beaten
150ml/5floz double cream

Place the sugar and water in a saucepan over a high heat and stir until the sugar dissolves. Bring to the boil and continue boiling, without stirring, until a syrup forms.

Meanwhile, melt the chocolate in the top of a double boiler, or in a heatproof bowl set over a pan of simmering water, stirring until it is smooth. Remove from the heat and briskly whisk in the sugar syrup. Return the mixture to the heat.

Blend the egg yolks and cream together, then whisk them into the chocolate sauce and simmer for about 8 minutes, whisking all the time, until the sauce thickens. Do not let the sauce boil or the eggs wills scramble.

Traditional Custard Sauce

Let's not forget the easy things in life! If the custard does become too hot and curdles, remove it from the heat and immediately whisk in another egg yolk. *Makes about 300ml/10fl oz.*

2 eggs yolks, size 3, lightly beaten
25g/1oz caster sugar
3 drops of vanilla essence
300ml/10floz milk, boiling
150ml/5fl oz double cream (optional)

Mix the egg yolks, sugar and vanilla essence in a large clean bowl. Whisk in the boiling milk, then return the custard to the saucepan over a low heat, stirring all the time with a wooden spoon until the custard becomes thick enough to coat the back of the spoon. Do not let the mixture boil or the eggs will scramble.

If you want extra creaminess, stir in the cream just before you take the custard off the heat. Serve at once, or leave to cool completely, cover and refrigerate for up to 2 days to serve chilled.

VARIATIONS
Christmas Brandy Custard Sauce Use the ingredients and method above, but omit the vanilla essence and stir in 3 tablespoons brandy.

Whisky or Rum Custard Sauce Omit the vanilla and stir in 2 tablespoons whisky or rum at the end of the simmering time and whisk gently together.

Chantilly Cream

Makes about 175ml/6fl oz.

150ml/5floz whipping cream
2 tablespoons caster sugar
1 tablespoon cream sherry

Whip the cream and sugar together in a chilled bowl until the cream begins to stiffen, then gently fold in the sherry. Serve immediately or cover and chill until required.

VARIATION

Fruity Chantilly Cream Purée or crush 50g/2oz of your favourite fruit and fold it into the chantilly cream.

Sabayon Sauce

This is the French version of Italian zabaglione, which is made with Marsala. *Makes about 400ml/14fl oz.*

4 egg yolks, size 3
100g/4oz caster sugar
300ml/10floz dry white wine, Madeira or milk

Put the egg yolks and sugar in a 1 litre/1¾ pint heatproof bowl and whisk together, then slowly whisk in the wine, Madeira or milk.

Place the bowl over a saucepan of gently simmering water, making sure the bottom of the bowl doesn't touch the water. Whisk the mixture continuously until it increases by volume and is firm and frothy.

Crème Pâtissière

I like to serve this with a rich chocolate soufflé. It can be served hot when it is freshly made, or be left to cool and then serve chilled. *Makes about 350ml/12fl oz.*

4 egg yolks, size 3
50g/2oz caster sugar
1 tablespoon plain flour
300ml/10fl oz milk, warm
1 teaspoon vanilla essence

Put the egg yolks and sugar into a clean large heatproof bowl and whisk together for 3 minutes.

Whisk in the flour, then gradually whisk in the milk and vanilla essence. Continue whisking until the mixture becomes smooth.

Place the mixture in the top of a double boiler or in a heatproof bowl over a saucepan of simmering water; do not let the bottom of the bowl touch the water. Stir until the sauce appears to be coming to the boil, then lower the heat and simmer for 3 minutes, stirring all the time. Pass the sauce through a fine sieve.

Icky Sticky Toffee Sponge with Toffee Sauce

No matter who I talk to about food and drink, I am almost always asked 'what is my favourite dessert?' That's easy to answer – Francis Coulson's Icky Sticky Toffee Sponge with Toffee Sauce from the renowned Sharrow Bay Country House Hotel, at Ullswater, in Cumbria. This is simple but truly delicious. *Serves 6.*

75g/6oz dates, chopped
150ml/5fl oz water
1 teaspoon bicarbonate of soda
50g/2oz best quality butter, softened
175g/6oz sugar
2 eggs, size 3, lightly beaten
175g/6oz self-raising flour
few drops of vanilla essence

for the toffee sauce
600ml/1 pint double cream
75g/3oz demerara sugar
1 tablespoon treacle

Preheat the oven to 180°C/350°F/gas mark 4. Put the dates, water and bicarbonate soda in a saucepan over a high heat and bring to the boil for 4 minutes.

Cream the butter and sugar together in a large bowl until light and fluffy. Gradually beat the eggs into the butter mixture, then add the flour, dates and their cooking liquid and the vanilla essence and fold together.

Spoon the mixture into a greased 20 × 15 × 10cm/8 × 6 × 4in loaf tin and bake for 45 minutes until it is firm.

Meanwhile, to make the sauce, put all the ingredients into a pan over a high heat and bring to the boil. Lower the heat and simmer for 10 minutes until reduced by one-quarter. Just before the end of the baking time, preheat the grill to high. Turn out the pudding onto a flameproof serving dish and pour the toffee sauce over the sponge. Hold the plate under the grill until the topping bubbles, then serve at once.

Old-fashioned English Butterscotch Sauce

Makes about 300ml/10fl oz.

225g/8oz light brown sugar
1 tablespoon golden syrup
50g/2oz butter
3 tablespoons double cream
1 teaspoon vanilla essence

Put the sugar and golden syrup in a saucepan over a medium heat and stir to dissolve the sugar. Add the butter and bring to the boil, then lower the heat and simmer for 10 minutes until the sauce is really thick. Remove the pan from the heat and stir in the cream and vanilla essence.

Rich Caramel Sauce

Makes about 200ml/7fl oz.

200g/7oz granulated sugar
125ml/4fl oz water

Put the granulated sugar and water in a saucepan over a high heat and stir to dissolve the sugar. Caramelize the mixture by bringing it to the boil and then simmering it, without stirring, for about 7 minutes until a clear caramel sauce forms. Remove the pan from the heat and set aside.

Mrs Raffald's Traditional Orange Sauce

Here's my version of this 1769 sauce from *The Experienced English Housekeeper*. This is ideal for transforming a light chocolate mousse or sponge cake into a special dessert. *Makes about 300ml/10fl oz.*

> finely shredded rind and juice of 2 large Seville oranges
> 2 tablespoons Cointreau or other orange-flavoured liqueur or brandy
> 100g/4oz caster sugar
> 3 egg yolks, size 3
> 300ml/10fl oz double cream

Put the orange rind and juice with just enough water to cover into a saucepan over a medium heat and simmer for 3 minutes to soften. Drain well and set aside.

Blend together the liqueur, sugar and egg yolks in a saucepan. Heat the double cream until almost at the boiling point, then pour it over the egg mixture, add the orange rind and whisk briskly.

Return the sauce to the pan over a low heat and simmer for 4 minutes, stirring all the time with a wooden spoon. Do not let the sauce boil or the eggs will scramble.

Grand Marnier Sauce

Makes about 300ml/10fl oz.

> 15g/½oz arrowroot
> 300ml/10fl oz freshly squeezed orange juice
> 25g/1oz caster sugar
> 50ml/2fl oz Grand Marnier or other orange-flavoured liqueur

Blend the arrowroot with 2 tablespoons of the orange juice.

Put the remaining orange juice and sugar into a saucepan and stir to dissolve the sugar, then bring to the boil. Lower the heat and simmer the orange juice over a very low heat. Add the arrowroot mixture and continue simmering over a low heat, stirring all the time, until the sauce thickens. Stir in the Grand Marnier or other liqueur.

Quick Orange Marmalade and Wine Sauce

Serve this hot with steamed puddings. *Makes about 150ml/5fl oz.*

> 6 tablespoons orange marmalade
> 2 tablespoons orange juice
> 5 tablespoons medium-dry white wine

Combine the marmalade, orange juice and wine in a saucepan over a medium heat and stir together. Simmer for about 6 minutes. Transfer to a sauce boat.

Quick Apricot and Orange Sauce

I spoon this sauce over ice cream and sweet soufflés. For a dessert fondue, present it with bite-size pieces of fruit for dipping into it. *Makes about 250ml/9fl oz.*

300g/10oz apricot jam
150ml/5fl oz orange juice
2 tablespoons kirsch
2 tablespoons Grand Marnier or other orange-flavoured liqueur

Put the apricot jam and orange juice into a saucepan over a high heat and stir to dissolve the jam. Bring to the boil, then lower the heat and simmer for 8 minutes. Stir in the kirsch and orange liqueur.

Suzette Sauce

Henri Charpentier (1880–1961) was a chef who is hardly mentioned in the cookery world, but as the inventor of this popular sauce he will never be forgotten by anyone who loves sauces, or the classic French dessert of *crêpes Suzette*.

As a food historian, it warms my heart every time I read his life story and his personal recipes. This world-famous sauce was accidentally invented while Charpentier was cooking for HRH The Prince of Wales (later Edward VII). It was obviously too long-winded to call the sauce The Prince of Wales Sauce, so instead he named it after the woman the prince was entertaining.

Charpentier advises that you make up 900g/2lb vanilla sugar in advance by putting four vanilla pods with the sugar into an air-tight jar. After three days the sugar will be delicately flavoured. About this sauce, he said: 'This can be made in advance and bottled; like good wine, it will improve with age.' *Makes enough for serving with 12 crêpes, or 4 portions.*

freshly squeezed juice of 2 oranges with the rinds cut into very fine strips
freshly squeezed juice of 1 lemon with the rind cut into very fine strips
4 tablespoons vanilla sugar (see above)
25g/1oz butter
1 tablespoon curaçao or other orange-flavoured liqueur
4 tablespoons kirsch
4 tablespoons white rum
4 tablespoons dark rum
2 tablespoons maraschino juice

for crêpes Suzette
12 prepared crêpes
kirsch

Blend the orange and lemon rinds with the sugar, then stir in the juices until the sugar dissolves.

Transfer the mixture to a saucepan over a medium heat with the butter and simmer for 1 minute until the butter melts, then stir in the remaining ingredients. Bring the sauce to the boil, then immediately remove from the heat and transfer the sauce to a sauce boat.

To make crêpes Suzette, fold the crêpes into triangles. Place the crêpes into a large frying pan and pour in a little of the sauce. When the sauce starts to bubble, add a generous tablespoon of warmed kirsch and set alight. Serve as soon as the flames dies down.

Sherry Sauce

Makes about 200ml/7fl oz.

150ml / 5fl oz milk
50g / 2oz sugar
50g / 2oz butter
3 tablespoons sweet sherry blended with
  1 tablespoon cornflour

Put the milk, sugar and butter in a saucepan over a high heat and stir to dissolve the sugar, then bring to the boil and boil for 5 minutes. Add the sherry and cornflour, lower the heat and simmer for 4 minutes, stirring all the time.

Sherry and Peach Cream Sauce

For something different this Christmas, try this with the steaming hot Christmas pudding. It's delicious. The sauce also looks stunning spooned over white peaches at other times of the year. *Makes about 300ml/10fl oz.*

25g / 1oz butter
25g / 1oz plain flour
300ml / 10fl oz cream sherry
4 tablespoons peach schnapps
2 tablespoons caster sugar
2 egg yolks, size 3, lightly beaten

Melt the butter in a saucepan over a medium heat, sprinkle in the flour and use a wooden spoon to stir together to form a roux. Gradually stir in the sherry and peach schnapps, then simmer for 3 minutes, stirring all the time.

Sprinkle in the sugar and stir until dissolved. Remove the pan from the heat and gradually whisk in the eggs. Return the sauce to the heat either in the top of a double boiler or in a heat-proof bowl set over a pan of gently simmering water and whisk constantly until the sauce is thick and smooth. Do not let the sauce boil or the eggs will scramble.

Rum or Brandy Sauce

Here's one of my favourite sauces for Christmas. I find Christmas sauces always bring out the worst in the cook, but the best in the people tasting the sauce. It really does no good for the cook to be tempted to say 'it's Christmas, so I'll double the amount' of spirit because it will only ruin the sauce. (Michael Smith, the former English cookery writer, used to make a delicious version of this using 3 tablespoons of Jamaican dark rum.) *Makes about 600ml/1 pint.*

50g / 2oz butter
25g / 1oz plain flour
600ml / 1 pint milk, warm
2 tablespoons caster sugar
3 tablespoons rum or brandy

Melt the butter in a saucepan over a medium heat, then sprinkle in the flour and use a wooden spoon to stir together to form a roux. Slowly stir in the warm milk, stirring all the time.

Sprinkle with the sugar and continue simmering for 8 minutes, stirring all the time. Add the rum or brandy and continue simmering for a further 5 minutes, stirring all the time to prevent the sauce sticking.

Your Own Favourite Liqueur Sauce

Flavour this sauce for serving with soufflés, hot fruit puddings and ice cream with your favourite liqueur. *Makes about 225ml/8fl oz.*

50g / 2oz butter, softened
75g / 3oz caster sugar
2 egg whites, size 3, beaten until just stiff and fluffy
150ml / 5fl oz double cream, whipped
4 tablespoons liqueur, such as brandy, Grand Marnier or Cointreau

Cream the butter and sugar together until light and fluffy, then slowly fold in the egg whites. Transfer the mixture to the top of a double boiler over a medium heat or to a heatproof bowl over a saucepan of simmering water; do not let the bottom of the bowl touch the water. Stir constantly until the mixture is heated through.

Remove the pan from the heat and fold in the whipped cream and the liqueur.

Eliza Acton's Wine Sauce for Sweet Puddings

Born in 1799 in Ipswich, Suffolk, Eliza Acton wrote *Modern Cooking in All its Branches* in 1845. Even after all these years, I find her recipes still work very well.

1. Boil gently together for 10 or 15 minutes the very thin rind of half a small lemon, about 2 ozs sugar and wineglassful of water.
2. Take out the lemon peel, and stir into the sauce 1 oz butter into which a large half-teaspoonful of flour has been smoothly kneaded.
3. Add a wineglassful and a half of sherry or Madeira, or other good white wine; and when quite hot serve the sauce without delay.

VARIATION
Port Wine Sauce
Use the ingredients and method as above, but substitute port for the white wine and add 1 tablespoon lemon juice, a little grated nutmeg and an extra 1 tablespoon caster sugar.

Hot Black Cherry Flambé Sauce

I make no apologies for using tinned cherries in this sauce – it's quicker than using fresh and the result tastes great. *Makes about 400g/14oz.*

25g/1oz butter
1 tin (410g/14oz) pitted black cherries in syrup, drained
75g/3oz caster sugar
3 tablespoons brandy, warmed

Melt the butter in a saucepan over a medium heat, add the cherries and cook them for 3 minutes, stirring occasionally. Sprinkle on the sugar and stir to dissolve, then transfer the hot cherries to a flameproof serving bowl. Pour over the warm brandy and set alight. Serve as soon as the flames die down.

Cherry Sauce

Makes about 400g/14oz.

1 tin (410g/14oz) pitted red cherries in syrup
50g/2oz caster sugar
2 tablespoons cornflour blended with 3 tablespoons reserved cherry syrup
25g/1oz butter
1 teaspoon lemon juice
few drops of almond essence

Drain the cherries, reserving 3 tablespoons of the syrup to blend with the cornflour, and pour the remaining syrup into a saucepan over a high heat. Bring the cherry syrup to the boil, then stir in the sugar, stirring until it dissolves. Simmer for a few minutes, then gradually stir in the cornflour mixture.

Slowly add the butter, lemon juice and almond essence and simmer for 1 minute. Serve using the cherries as the garnish.

Hot Coffee Sauce

I suggest serving this with rich chocolate cake. *Makes about 200ml/7fl oz.*

75g/3oz caster sugar
2 egg yolks, size 3
4 tablespoons cold, strong black coffee
150ml/5fl oz double cream
pinch of salt
vanilla essence

Whisk the sugar and egg yolks together in the top of a double boiler over a medium heat, or in a heatproof bowl on top of a pan of gently simmering water; do not let the bottom of the bowl touch the water.

Slowly add the coffee, whisking all the time. Add the double cream and salt and let the heat get to the cream, whisking constantly until the sauce thickens. Add a few drops of vanilla essence. Serve immediately in a sauce boat.

VARIATIONS

Hot Brandy Sauce Use the ingredients and method as for the coffee sauce, but omit the coffee and stir in 2 tablespoons brandy with the vanilla.

Hot Mocha Sauce Use the ingredients and method as for the coffee sauce, but add 100g/4oz melted dark chocolate with the sugar and eggs.

Ginger Sauce

Makes about 300ml/10fl oz.

300ml/10floz traditional custard sauce (page 100)
1 teaspoon ground ginger
1 tablespoon golden syrup
lemon juice

Heat the custard sauce, then whisk in the ginger and sweeten with the syrup. Add lemon juice to taste.

Lemon Sauce

Makes about 100ml/4fl oz.

25g/1oz butter
75g/3oz caster sugar
1 egg yolk
2 tablespoons lemon juice
1 tablespoon dry sherry
2 egg whites, size 3, beaten until stiff

Cream the butter in the top of a double boiler or a large heatproof bowl until light and fluffy. Slowly beat in the sugar, beating until it dissolves, then whisk in the egg yolk, lemon juice and sherry.

Place the double boiler over medium heat or place the bowl over a saucepan of simmering water. Heat the mixture for 5 minutes, whisking constantly. Remove the pan or bowl from the heat and fold in the beaten egg whites.

VARIATION

Strawberry-lemon Sauce Use the same ingredients and method, adding 75g/3oz crushed strawberries and 1 tablespoon kirsch when you fold in the beaten egg whites.

Marshmallow Sauce

This is a classic American sauce for spooning over ice cream that I first enjoyed while working and travelling across the States. *Makes about 225ml/8fl oz.*

100g/4oz caster sugar
pinch of salt
75ml/3floz water, boiling
150g/5oz marshmallows (about 16 large ones), chopped
1 teaspoon vanilla essence
2 egg whites, size 3, beaten until firm

Place the sugar, salt and boiling water in a saucepan over a medium heat, stirring until the sugar dissolves, then slowly bring the syrup to the boil. Lower the heat and simmer for 6 minutes.

Slowly stir the marshmallows into the syrup, stirring until they melt, then stir in the vanilla essence. Pour the hot syrup slowly on to the beaten egg whites, folding gently until the sauce is smooth.

Melba Sauce

Makes about 175ml/6fl oz.

4 tablespoons redcurrant jelly
100g / 4oz raspberries, crushed to a purée
50g / 2oz caster sugar
1 teaspoon cornflour
1 tablespoon water

Melt the redcurrant jelly in a saucepan over a high heat, stir in the raspberries and bring to the boil. Lower the heat and simmer for 2 minutes, stirring occasionally.

Stir the sugar, cornflour and water together, then gradually whisk the mixture into the sauce, whisking until the sauce thickens.

I really am sorry this book must come to an end, but for your interest my last recipe is a little gem from Elizabeth Raffald in *The Experienced English Housekeeper* (1769). I am sure you will enjoy this. Remember that the letter *f* represents the letter *s*.

To make a SYLLABUB under the COW

PUT a bottle of ftrong-beer and a pint of cyder into a punch bowl, grate in a fmall nutmeg, and befweeten it to your tafte; then milk as much milk from the cow as will make a ftrong froth, and the ale look clear, let it ftand an hour, and ftrew over it a few currants, well wafhed, picked and plumped before the fire, and fend to the table.

Useful Terms and Techniques

Bain-marie This term describes a method of cooking by indirect heat, as well as a specific piece of equipment. The cooking pot, bowl or pan is set inside a larger pan containing simmering water. The hot water can then be used to cook the sauce or keep it hot.

Beating A whipping motion, using a fork, whisk or beater, to introduce air into the mixture to make it smooth and light.

Beurre manie Equal amounts of butter and flour creamed together, which are then added to hot liquids to thicken them.

Blanch To pre-heat in hot water for a short time to soften or to remove any strongly flavoured elements.

Blend To combine two or more ingredients thoroughly by mixing them together with a beating or stirring motion.

Boil To heat liquids so the temperature increases continuously, causing bubbles to rise to the surface.

Bouilli An abbreviation of the French term *boeuf boulli*, or boiled beef. The liquid in which the meat has been boiled. The expression 'bully beef' derives from it.

Bouquet garni A bunch of herbs, placed in a muslin and tied. It is put into the sauce while cooking to give flavour, and is taken out before serving. Most bouquet garnis contain bay leaf, thyme, sage, parsley, peppercorns and a clove of garlic, but other simple herb combinations can be used. You can also buy these in sachets that look like tea bags.

Caramelize To heat sugar slowly, without any added liquid, until it dissolves and takes on a golden brown colour.

Clarify To clear the scum and milky froth from butter, so it can be cooked at a higher temperature without burning. Or, to clear the surface of a stock. A very good tip to clarify stocks is to add the crushed egg shell with a lightly beaten egg white. The egg shell attracts any particles in the liquid, which are then 'trapped' in the egg white as it congeals.

Coulis In English this term means a purée or thick sauce, very often made from fruits, such as strawberries, blackberries or tomatoes. It was once, however, the word applied to all French sauces.

Dégraisser To remove the fat from the surface of the sauces.

Depouiller une sauce To skim a sauce to remove all impurities as they rise during cooking.

Fines herbes Savoury combinations of herbs, similar to bouquet garnis. The classic combination is parsley, chervil, chives and tarragon.

Folding A method of combining beaten egg whites or whipped cream with another mixture so that the air cells are not broken down. This helps to keep the mixture light.

Julienne To cut ingredients, usually vegetables, into very fine strips, like matchsticks. I use many vegetables prepared in this way throughout this book.

Marinade The liquid in which meat, poultry, fish or game is soaked to tenderize it, add flavour or, especially in the case of game, preserve it if it cannot be cooked at once. Usually contains wine vinegar, olive oil, herbs and seasoning.

Mirepoix A mixture of finely diced vegetables sautéed in butter and used to flavour other sauce ingredients.

Purée Cooked or raw food which has been pushed through a fine sieve or liquefied in a blender or food processor.

Reduce A sauce is reduced by boiling so it thickens as stock or other liquids evaporate; this process also reduces the volume. The mark of a good sauce-maker is knowing when a sauce is properly reduced.

Roux A slowly, but thoroughly, cooked mixture of fat and flour that is used as a thickener. There are three colour tones for a roux, determined by the length of cooking and amount of browning, which are white, blond and brown (see page 23).

Sauté To cook and brown lightly in a small amount of fat. In English, this is often called pan frying.

Scald To heat liquids until bubbles form, but before boiling point is reached.

Skimming To remove any foam or scum that rises to the surface when boiling. This foam carries to the surface all the impurities and should be removed slowly and gently and at regular intervals. Do not boil furiously.

Useful Herbs and Spices

Here are the herbs and spices I use in my recipes. You will find them in supermarkets and delicatessens

Allspice Also known as Jamaican pepper, this spice's name is derived from its flavour, which resembles a combination of cinnamon, cloves and nutmeg. It gives a fragrant and pungent aroma

Aniseed This has been used since the time of Henry III to flavour creams and cakes and to add colour to food.

Balm Also known as lemon balm or sweet balm, this goes well with fish and is used to add colour to food.

Basil Used widely in Italian and French cookery, basil has a warm, spicy taste. It is the essential ingredient in pesto sauce (page 87) and often features in other pasta sauces. The essential oil obtained from the plant contains camphor, which is believed to prevent throat infections.

Bay One of the classic ingredients of bouquet garni, bay adds a delicate flavour to casseroles, soups and game dishes.

Bouquet garni The routine bouquet, or faggot (as a bundle was once called), of herbs is used to flavour most soups and stews. I include it in my meat stock recipe (page 20). Contents vary, but they usually include a bay leaf, three sprigs of parsley with their stalks and one sprig of thyme, tied together with a long thread so that they can be pulled out when the dish is cooked. The French often include a crushed clove of garlic in Provençal cooking.

Caraway seed Often used in pork and veal dishes, caraway seed is a favourite addition to sauerkraut

Chervil This is a popular addition to omelettes and salads in France, where it is known as *pluches de cerfeuil*. The herb, which was introduced to Britain by the Romans, has a more delicate, elusive flavour than parsley, and I make more use of it by adding it to parsley sauce The leaves are plucked from the stem, rather than chopped.

Chives Use as a garnish for onion sauce.

Cloves This important spice is classified as a flower spice because it is the dried, unopened bud of a tropical tree. It is rich in essential oils and characterized by a sweet, strong, pungent aroma and flavour. Use in béchamel sauce (page 26) and for studding ham and pork before they are cooked. I include some in my traditional bread sauce recipe on page 49.

Coriander The dried seeds of the coriander plant have an aromatic and slightly orange scent, and they were at one time used to flavour sweet creams. Today, they are mostly used in Indian-style sauces.

Cumin seed The strong aromatic taste is both hot and bitter and an essential ingredient for Indian-style sauces. It is also used occasionally in the cookery of Alsace. See the curry powder recipe on pages 51–2.

Dill The delicate-looking sprigs of dill are often used to garnish sauces and fish dishes, and the seeds, which have a pleasant, pungent, aromatic flavour, are frequently used as a condiment with vinegars and for flavouring cakes. William the Conqueror's cook, Tezlin, made a white cream soup called 'dillegrout', which he flavoured and garnished with chopped fresh dill.

Fennel seed One of my favourite spices for barbecues, the seeds look like watermelon seeds. They exude a warm, sweet and pleasant anise flavour. Several hundred years ago fennel tea was made by pouring 300ml/10fl oz boiling water over 1 teaspoon of the seeds, then leaving the mixture to infuse for 5 minutes.

Garlic Like chives, leeks and shallots, this pungent herb is a member of the onion family. It originates from central Asia, not France as many people believe. Cookery would not be the same without it.

Ginger Used in the time of Henry III, this full-flavoured spice was not seen for 200 years, and then was reintroduced by the Dutch in 1565. It has been included in gingerbread recipes since the 14th century, but I like to make it into a syrup to serve with fresh melon.

Herbes de Provence As the name implies, this is a staple of Provençal cooking. The herbs usually include savory, marjoram, oregano, thyme, rosemary, basil and tarragon.

Horseradish This is, of course, the main ingredient of the sauce of the same name that is served with meat dishes around the world. Fresh horseradish sauce is far superior to the bottled version that is sold in supermarkets throughout Britain and that is overpowered with stabilizers and artificial colourings. I add cream to my recipe (page 53) to make a first class sauce; see also kren sauce (page 66).

Marjoram A herb with a sweet, pleasant and delicate flavour, which is excellent in sauces and soups. This was particularly popular during the reign of Elizabeth I.

Mint Known as the herb of Venus, this is the ideal and traditional accompaniment for roast lamb. I use mint fresh from my garden to make mint sauce (page 54) and apple and mint sorbet.

Mustard seed These tiny seeds – brown, black or yellow – are the essential ingredient in mustard. Most countries have their own mustard recipe, such as the hot and full-flavoured English mustard and Dijon mustard from France. The mustard sauce (page 29) is an ideal accompaniment to roast meat; see also the mild mustard sauce (page 31).

Nutmeg This popular spice was used in virtually everything in the nineteenth century. I use it to flavour vegetable sauces and soups.

Oregano Use this highly aromatic and pungent herb with discretion. It is especially popular in Greek, Mexican and Italian cookery.

Parsley A familiar herb and a staple ingredient in several sauces as well as a popular garnish, parsley was introduced to Britain in 1548. It is said that if you chew parsley after you have eaten garlic, the parsley will remove the smell of garlic from your breath. A *persillade* in French cookery is a mixture of finely chopped parsley with shallot or garlic, added as a flavouring during the final stages of cooking vegetable and meat dishes. See parsley sauce (page 25).

Peppercorns Known as the world's most valuable spice, freshly milled black or white peppercorns are two of the most important ingredients in sauce cookery. You will find freshly milled pepper is far superior to shop-bought ground pepper, so I urge you to use your peppermill in every aspect of cookery. An overwhelming peppery taste in many English dishes, especially the English sausage, is the result of inferior ground pepper rather than freshly milled peppercorns.

Rosemary This is excellent for flavouring lamb while it roasts and for mixing with apple to serve with pork. Yet the flavour is much too strong to use on its own in a sauce – use rosemary with a light hand in all cookery.

Saffron The stigmas of *Crocus sativus* yield this exotic substance, which is the most expensive spice in the world. It has been estimated that 480,000 pistils – about 165,000 flowers – are required to make 1kg/2lb of dried saffron, which explains not only why it is so expensive but also why it is so often faked. Before it is used, the strands are usually finely ground or crumbled and left to infuse in hot water. The golden liquid that results is used to flavour and colour sauces and boiled rice.

Sage Traditionally included in chicken, duck, goose and pork stuffings, this perennial herb is a member of the nettle family.

Savory Use this herb in egg dishes and in sauces and as a garnish.

Tansy This is an old-fashioned herb that is used to flavour soup and sauces and to garnish salads.

Tarragon A herb that originates from Siberia and northwest America, tarragon is excellent for including in sauces and salads, and it makes a brilliantly flavoured vinegar – use a little tarragon vinegar to flavour the apple sauce recipe on page 49. Tarragon is also one of the traditional ingredients in a classic Béarnaise sauce (see page 32), and I include it in a traditional tarragon and lemon sauce from Portugal (page 90).

Thyme Fresh thyme is one of the most underrated herbs. As well as adding flavour when it is rubbed into meat with a little salt and oil, thyme helps to tenderize the flesh while it cooks.

Further Reading

Acton, Eliza, *Modern Cooking in All its Branches*, 1845

The Art of Cookery, Made Plain and Easy, By a Lady, 1747

Audot, Louis Eustache, *La Cuisinière des Villes et des Campagnes*, 1818

Beeton, Mrs Isabella, *The Book of Household Management*, Ward Lock, 1861

Bridge, Tom, *The Golden Age of Cookery*, Ross Anderson Publications, 1982

Bridge, Tom and Cooper-English, Colin, *Dr William Kitchiner, A Regency Eccentric: Author of 'The Cook's Oracle'*, Southover Press, 1993

Brown, Professor O. Phelps, *The Complete Herbalist*, Frederick W. Hale, 1907

Charpentier, Henri, *The Henri Charpentier Cookbook*, Price, Stern, Sloan, 1970

Contarini, Paolo, *The Savoy was My Oyster*, Robert Hale, 1976

Drewery, George, M.D., *Common Sense Management of the Stomach*, 1875

Eaton, Mrs Mary, *The Cook and Householder's Complete and Universal Dictionary*, 1823

Escoffier, Auguste, *The Complete Guide to the Art of Modern Cookery*, Flammarion, 1921 and Heinemann, 1986

Farley, John, *The London Art of Cookery*, 1783 (reprinted Southover Press, 1988)

Francatelli, Charles Elmé, *The Cook's Guide*, Bentley, 1869

Glasse, Hannah, *The Art of Cookery*, 1747

Gouffe, Jules, *Royal Cookery Book*, 1869

Jewry, Mary, *Warne's Model Cookery and Housekeeping Book*, 1868

Kettner, Auguste, *The Book of the Table*, 1877 (reprinted Centaur Press, 1968)

Kitchiner, Dr William, *The Cook's Oracle*, 1817

Marshall, Mrs Agnes, *Cookery Book*, 1888

Oliver, Raymond, *Gastronomy of France*, World Publishing Co., 1970

Raffald, Elizabeth, *The Experienced English Housekeeper*, 1796

Rundle, Mrs, *A New System of Domestic Cookery*, 1846

Simon, André L., *Guide to Good Food and Wines*, 1949

Simon, André L., *Basic English Fare*, 1960

Soyer, Alexis, *The Modern Housewife or Managère*, 1853

White, Florence, *Good Things in England*, Jonathan Cape, 1933

The Young Woman's Companion or Frugal Housewife, Russell & Allen, 1811

Index of Sauces

Vinegars
Herb Vinegars 16
Honey and Caper Vinegar 15
Lemon and Black Peppercorn
    Vinegar 15
Lemon Vinegar 15
Orange and Green Peppercorn
    Vinegar 15
Raspberry Vinegar 15
Rose Petal Vinegar 16

Stocks
Chicken Stock 21
Court Bouillon 20
Fish Stock 19
Game Stock 22
Meat Stock 20–21
Veal Stock 21
Vegetable Stock 22

Roux
Blond Roux 23
Brown Roux 23
White Roux 23

Basic Sauces
Anchovy Sauce 25
Béchamel Sauce 26
Bercy Sauce 27–8
Breton Sauce 27
Caper Sauce 25
Chaudfroid Sauce 27
Chivry Sauce 27
Diplomat Sauce 27
Herb Sauce 25
Italian Rich Cheese Sauce 26
Mornay Sauce 25
Mushroom Sauce 25, 27
Normandy Sauce 27
Onion or Shallot Sauce 25

Parsley Sauce 25
Rich Cheese Sauce 25–6
Sauce Allemande 27
Sauce Parisienne 27
Sauce Ravigote 27
Sauce Riche 27
Sauce Talleyrande 27
Shrimp Sauce 26
Velouté Sauce 26
White Fish Sauce 26
White Sauce 25

Melted Butter Sauces
Beurre Blanc 29
Beurre Noir 29
Beurre Noisette 29
Black Butter Sauce 29
Butter Sauce 29
Egg Sauce 29
Mustard Sauce 29
Parsley and Butter Sauce 28–9
Sauce Polonaise 29

Savoury and Herb Butters
Garlic Butter 30
Lobster Butter 30
Maître d'Hôtel 30
Parsley Butter 30
Shrimp Butter 30
Tromp's Lobster Butter 30
Watercress Butter 30

Egg Sauces
Aïoli 34
Avocado Mystique 34
Bavarois Sauce 32
Béarnaise Sauce 32
Beetroot Mayonnaise 34
Bridge Sauce 33
Chaudfroid Sauce 34

Coronation Chicken Sauce 34
Hollandaise Sauce 31
Lobster Newburg Sauce 32
Maltaise Sauce 31
Mayonnaise 33–4
Mild Mustard Sauce 31
Mousseline Sauce 31
Mustard Mayonnaise 34
Rich Mousseline Sauce 32
Russian Sauce 34
Sauce Choron 33
Sauce Fayot 33
Sauce Louis 34
Sauce Paloise 33
Sauce Rémoulade 34

Demi-glace Sauces
Bordelaise Sauce 35
Demi-glace Sauce 35
Devilled Sauce 37
Espagnole Sauce 38–9
Hunters' Sauce 36
Madeira Sauce 35
Pepper Sauce 37–8, 39
Quick Chicken, Hunters' Style 36
Red Wine Demi-glace Sauce 35
Rich Madeira Sauce 35
Sauce Bigarade 39
Sauce Diane 38
Sauce Piquante 38

Wine Sauces
Bordelaise Sauce 40
Sauce Bourguignonne 40

Famous English Sauces
Harvey's Sauce 41–2
Oyster Sauce for Roast Shoulder of
    Mutton 43
Pigeon Sauce 43

Sauce for Any Land Fowl, Game or
  Turkey 43
Sauce for Pork, Goslings, Chicken,
  Lamb or Kid 43
Sauce for Roast Shoulder of Mutton
  without Oysters 43
Worcestershire Sauce 44

Gravy and Brown Sauce
Brown Onion Sauce 46
Liver, Bacon and Onions with Brown
  Onion Sauce 46
Perfect Gravy 44–5
Tomato Sauce 45

Game Sauces
Cumberland Sauce 47
My Grandmother's Suet Pastry 48
Old English Game Sauce 47
Rosa's Quail Pudding 48

Traditional English Sauces
American Shrimp Sauce 54
Apple Sauce 49
Beauvilliers' Receipt for Sauce Robert
  57
Bread Sauce 49
Cardinal Sauce 54
Chestnut Sauce 50
Cranberry Sauce 50
Currant Sauce 51
Curry Sauce 51–2
Gooseberry Sauce 52
Ham Sauce 52
Horseradish Sauce 53
Lobster Sauce 53–4
Mint Sauce 54
Mr Michael Kelly's Sauce 58
Mushroom Sauce 54
Redcurrant Sauce 55
Reform Sauce 55
Roast Beef Sauce 53
Robert Sauce 56
Sauce aux Cevettes 54
Sauce Charcutière 56
Sauce for Stewed or Bouilli Beef
  58
Sauce for Tripe or Cow-heel or
  Calf's Head 58
Sauce Poulette 54
Sultana Sauce 51
Tartare Sauce 57

Wow-wow Sauce 58

International and Modern Sauces
AMERICA
All-American Tomato Sauce 59
Californian Sherry Sauce 60
Carib Paradise Island Sauce 63
Champagne Sauce 60
Chicken on Her Nest 59
Cider Sauce for Baked Ham 60
Hot Creole Sauce 60
Hot and Spicy Green Tomato Sauce
  61
Millionaires' Oyster Sauce 61
Oyster Sauce 61
Pacific Pineapple Sauce 62
Pacific Prawn Sauce 62
Paradise Sauce 63
Prune Sauce 63
San Francisco Barbecue Sauce 64
Sweet and Sour Sauce 62
Texas Tomato Sauce 59
White Wine, Honey and Garlic
  Marinade . . . and Sauce 64

AUSTRALIA
Hake with Fresh Herb, Tomato and
  Wine Sauce 65
Lemon Grass, Orange and Coconut
  Sauce 65

AUSTRIA
Dill Sauce 66
Honey, Mustard and Poppy Seed
  Sauce 66
Kren Sauce 66
Mackerel with Horseradish Sauce 66

BELGIUM
Sauce Roeselare, Francis Carroll Style
  67

CARIBBEAN
Mango and Papaya Sauce 68
Papaya Mustard Sauce 68–9
Papaya Sauce 68
Sofrito Sauce 69
Sweet and Sour Pineapple Sauce 69

CHINA
Black Bean Sauce 70
Cho Low Yu 71

La Fu Jiang 70
Lung Ha Jiang 71
Ngo Pa Tsup 72
Op Tsup 72

ENGLAND
Nut Sauce 73
Port and Pink Peppercorn Sauce 73
Rose Petal and Honey Sauce for
  Wild Breast of Duckling 73
Royal Lamb Korma 74
Stilton Sauce 74

FRANCE
Duckling with Breton Cider Sauce 75
Sauce Gibier 76
Sauce Périgueux 77
Sauce Rossini 77
Sauce Vierge 76
Steak Rossini 77
Truffle Sauces 77

GERMANY
Fresh Ox Tongue with Raisin Sauce
  78
German Game Sauce 78

GREECE
Egg and Lemon Sauce 79
Moussaka 79
Skorthalia 80

HUNGARY
Veal Cutlets with Paprika Sauce
  81

INDIA
Beef Korma 82

IRELAND
A Very Good Irish Sauce 83
Beef with Guinness Sauce 83
Pears in a Wild Mint Vinaigrette
  84

ITALY
Bolognese Sauce 85
Bulgare Sauce 86
Byron Sauce 86
Genovese Sauce for Fish 85
Marsala Sauce 87
Pesto Sauce 87

Sauce Colbert 87
Sauce Czardas 86
Sauce Françoise 86
Sauce Italienne 86
Tomato and Beef Sauce 86
Tomato Sauce 87

JAPAN
Prawns with Peanut Sauce 88

NEW ZEALAND
Lamb Fillet with Kiwi Sauce 89
Lime Sauce 89

PORTUGAL
Lemon and Tarragon Sauce 90
Loin of Veal, Portuguese Style 90
Olive Sauce 91
Salsa Pizzaiola 91
Sauce for Loin of Pork 91

SCANDINAVIA
Danish Blue Cheese Sauce 92
Dill Sas 92

SPAIN
Canary Island Red Sauce 93
Green Sauce 93
Olive Sauce 93
Pine Nut Sauce 93

THAILAND
Pork Curry 94

Fondue Sauces
Fondue Bourguignonne 95
Gruyère Sauce 95
Luxury Swiss Fondue Sauce 96

Dressings and Dips
French Dressing 97
Guacamole Dip 97
Honey and Lemon Dressing 97
Sour Cream and Dill Dip 97
Tomato and Garlic Dressing 97
Tomato, Honey and Lemon Dressing 97

Dessert Sauces
Chantilly Cream 101
Cherry Sauce 107
Christmas Brandy Custard Sauce 100
Crème Pâtissière 101
Eliza Acton's Wine Sauce for Sweet Puddings 106
Fruity Chantilly Cream 101
Ginger Sauce 108
Grand Marnier Sauce 103
Hot Black Cherry Flambé Sauce 107
Hot Brandy Sauce 107
Hot Coffee Sauce 107
Hot Mocha Sauce 107
Icky Sticky Toffee Sponge with Toffee Sauce 102
Lemon Sauce 108
Luxury Chocolate Sauce 100

Marshmallow Sauce 108
Melba Sauce 108
Mrs Raffald's Traditional Orange Sauce 103
Old-fashioned English Butterscotch Sauce 102
Port Wine Sauce 106
Quick Apricot and Orange Sauce 104
Quick Chocolate Sauce 100
Quick Orange Marmalade and Wine Sauce 103
Quick Sweet Almond Sauce 99
Quick Sweet Chocolate Sauce
Quick Sweet Coffee Sauce 99
Quick Sweet Ginger Sauce 99
Quick Sweet Liqueur Sauce 99
Quick Sweet Rum and Raisin Sauce 99
Quick Sweet White Sauce 99
Rich Caramel Sauce 102
Rum or Brandy Sauce 105
Rum Custard Sauce
Sabayon Sauce 101
Sherry and Peach Cream Sauce 105
Sherry Sauce 105
Strawberry-lemon Sauce 108
Suzette Sauce 104
Traditional Custard Sauce 100
Whisky Custard Sauce 100
Your Own Favourite Liqueur Sauce 106

General Index

Aïoli 34
All-American Tomato Sauce 59
Allemande, Sauce 27
Almond Sauce, Quick Sweet 99
American
   Sauces 59–64
   Shrimp Sauce 54
Anchovy Sauce 25
Apple Sauce 49
Apricot and Orange Sauce, Quick
   104
Australian Sauces 65
Austrian Sauces 66
Avocado Mystique 34

Bacon and Onions, Liver, with
   Brown Onion Sauce 46
Baked Ham, Cider Sauce for 60
Barbecue Sauce, San Francisco 64
Basic Sauces 25–8
Bavarois Sauce 32
Bean Sauce, Black 70
Béarnaise Sauce 32
Beauvilliers' Receipt for Sauce Robert
   57
Béchamel Sauce 26
Beef
   Guinness Sauce, with 83
   Korma 82
   Roast Beeef Sauce 53
   Sauce for Stewed or Bouilli Beef 58
   Tomato and Beef Sauce 86
Beetroot Mayonnaise 34
Belgian Sauces 67
Bercy Sauce 27–8
Beurre
   Blanc 29
   Noir 29
   Noisette 29
Bigarade, Sauce 39

Black
   Bean Sauce 70
   Butter Sauce 29
   Cherry Flambé Sauce, Hot 107
   Peppercorn Vinegar, Lemon and
     15
Blanc, Beurre 29
Blond Roux 23
Bolognese Sauce 85
Bordelaise Sauce 35, 40
Bourguignonne
   Fondue 95
   Sauce 40
Brandy
   Custard Sauce, Christmas 100
   Sauce 105
   Sauce, Hot 107
Bread Sauce 49
Breton
   Cider Sauce, Duckling with 75
   Sauce 27
Bridge Sauce 33
Brown
   Onion Sauce 46
   Roux 23
   Sauce, Gravy and 44–6
Bulgare Sauce 86
Butter
   Garlic 30
   Lobster 30
   Parsley 30
   Sauce 29
   Sauce, Black 29
   Sauce, Parsley and 28–9
   Sauces, Melted 28–9
   Shrimp 30
   Tromp's Lobster 30
   Watercress 30
Butterscotch Sauce, Old-fashioned
   English 102

Byron Sauce 86

Calf's Head, Sauce for Tripe or
   Cow-heel or 58
Californian Sherry Sauce 60
Canary Island Red Sauce 93
Caper
   Sauce 25
   Vinegar, Honey and 15
Caramel Sauce, Rich 102
Cardinal Sauce 54
Carib Paradise Island Sauce 63
Caribbean Sauces 68–9
Cevettes, Sauce aux 54
Champagne Sauce 60
Chantilly Cream 101
   Fruity 101
Charcutière, Sauce 56
Chaudfroid Sauce 27, 34
Cheese
   Saucc, Danish Blue 92
   Sauce, Italian Rich 26
   Sauce, Rich 25–6
Cherry
   Flambé Sauce, Hot Black 107
   Sauce 107
Chestnut Sauce 50
Chicken
   on Her Nest 59
   Quick, Hunters' Style 36
   Sauce, Coronation 34
   Stock 21
Chinese Sauces 70–2
Chivry Sauce 27
Cho Low Yu 71
Chocolate Sauce
   Luxury 100
   Quick 100
   Quick Sweet 99
Choron, Sauce 33

Christmas Brandy Custard Sauce 100
Cider Sauce
  Baked Ham, for 60
  Duckling with Breton 75
Coconut Sauce, Lemon Grass,
  Orange and 65
Coffee Sauce
  Hot 107
  Quick Sweet 99
Colbert, Sauce 87
Cooking Oils 19
Coronation Chicken Sauce 34
Court Bouillon 20
Cow-heel or Calf's Head, Sauce for
  Tripe or 58
Cranberry Sauce 50
Cream
  Chantilly 101
  Fruity Chantilly 101
  Sauce, Sherry and Peach 105
Crème Pâtissière 101
Creole Sauce, Hot 60
Cumberland Sauce 47
Currant Sauce 51
Curry
  Pork 94
  Sauce 51–2
Custard Sauce
  Christmas Brandy 100
  Rum 100
  Traditional 100
  Whisky 100
Czardas, Sauce 86

Danish Blue Cheese Sauce 92
Demi-glace Sauces 35–9
  Red Wine 35
Dessert Sauces 99–109
Devilled Sauce 37
d'Hôtel, Maître 30
Diane, Sauce 38
Dill
  Dip, Sour Cream and 97
  Sas 92
  Sauce 66
Dip
  Guacamole 97
  Sour Cream and Dill 97
Diplomat Sauce 27
Dressing
  French 97
  Honey and Lemon 97

Tomato and Garlic 97
Tomato, Honey and Lemon 97
Dressings and Dips 97
Duckling
  Breton Cider Sauce, with 75
  Rose Petal and Honey Sauce for
    Wild Breast of 73

Egg
  Lemon Sauce, and 79
  Sauce 29
  Sauces 31–4
Eliza Acton's Wine Sauce for Sweet
  Puddings 106
English
  Butterscotch Sauce, Old-fashioned
    102
  Game Sauce, Old 47
  Sauces 41–4, 49–58, 73–4
Espagnole Sauce 38–9

Famous English Sauces 41–4
Favourite Liqueur Sauce, Your Own
  106
Fayot Sauce 33
Fish
  Genovese Sauce for 85
  Sauce, White 26
  Stock 19
Fondue
  Bourguignonne 95
  Sauce, Luxury Swiss 96
  Sauces 95
Fowl, Game or Turkey Sauce for
  Any Land 43
Francis Carroll Style, Sauce Roeselare
  67
Françoise, Sauce 86
French
  Dressing 97
  Sauces 75–7
Fresh
  Herb Tomato and Wine Sauce,
    Hake with 65
  Ox Tongue with Raisin Sauce 78
Fruity Chantilly Cream 101

Game
  Sauce, German 78
  Sauce, Old English 47
  Sauces 47–8
  Stock 22

Garlic
  Butter 30
  Dressing, Tomato and 97
  Marinade, White Wine, Honey
    and . . . and Sauce 64
  Oil 18
Genovese Sauce for Fish 85
German
  Game Sauce 78
  Sauces 78
Gibier, Sauce 76
Ginger Sauce 108
  Quick Sweet 99
Gooseberry Sauce 52
Grand Marnier Sauce 103
Gravy
  Brown Sauce, and 44–6
  Perfect 44–5
Greek Sauces 79–80
Green
  Peppercorn Vinegar, Orange and
    17
  Tomato Sauce, Hot and Spicy 61
  Sauce 93
Gruyère Sauce 95
Guacamole Dip 97
Guinness Sauce, Beef with 83

Hake with Fresh Herb, Tomato and
  Wine Sauce 65
Ham
  Baked, Cider Sauce for 60
  Sauce 52
Harvey's Sauce 41–2
Herb
  Butters, Savoury and 30
  Sauce 25
  Tomato and Wine Sauce, Hake
    with Fresh 65
  Vinegars 16
Hollandaise Sauce 31
Honey
  Caper Vinegar, and 15
  Garlic Marinade, White Wine, and
    . . . and Sauce 64
  Lemon Dressing, and 97
  Lemon Dressing, Tomato and
    97
  Mustard and Poppy Seed Sauce
    66
  Sauce for Wild Breast of Duckling,
    Rose Petal and 73

Horseradish Sauce 53
  Mackerel with 66
Hot
  Black Cherry Flambé Sauce 107
  Brandy Sauce 107
  Coffee Sauce 107
  Creole Sauce 60
  Mocha Sauce 107
  Spicy Green Tomato Sauce, and 61
Hungarian Sauces 81
Hunters'
  Sauce 36
  Style, Quick Chicken 36

Icky Sticky Toffee Sponge with
  Toffee Sauce 102
Indian Sauces 82
Irish
  Sauce, A Very Good 83
  Sauces 83–4
Italian
  Rich Cheese Sauce 26
  Sauces 85–7
Italienne, Sauce 86

Japanese Sauces 88

Kelly's Sauce, Mr Michael 58
Kiwi Sauce, Lamb Fillet with 89
Korma
  Beef 82
  Royal Lamb 74
Kren Sauce 66

La Fu Jiang 70
Lamb
  Fillet with Kiwi Sauce 89
  Korma, Royal 74
Lemon
  Black Peppercorn Vinegar, and 15
  Dressing, Honey and 97
  Dressing, Tomato, Honey and 97
  Grass, Orange and Coconut Sauce
    65
  Sauce, Egg and 79
  Sauce 108
  Tarragon Sauce, and 90
  Vinegar 15
Lime Sauce 89
Liqueur Sauce
  Quick Sweet 99
  Your Own Favourite 106

Liver, Bacon and Onions with Brown
  Onion Sauce 46
Lobster
  Butter 30
  Butter, Tromp's 30
  Newburg Sauce 32
  Sauce 53–4
Loin of
  Pork, Sauce for 91
  Veal, Portuguese Style 90
Louis, Sauce 34
Lung Ha Jiang 71
Luxury
  Chocolate Sauce 100
  Swiss Fondue Sauce 96

Mackerel with Horseradish Sauce 66
Madeira Sauce 35
  Rich 35
Maître d'Hôtel 30
Maltaise Sauce 31
Mango and Papaya Sauce 68
Marsala Sauce 87
Marshmallow Sauce 108
Mayonnaise 33–4
  Beetroot 34
  Mustard 34
Meat Stock 20–21
Melba Sauce 109
Melted Butter Sauces 28–9
Mild Mustard Sauce 31
Millionaires' Oyster Sauce 61
Mint
  Sauce 54
  Vinaigrette, Pears in a Wild 84
Mocha Sauce, Hot 107
Mock Smoked Salmon 18
Mornay Sauce 25
Moussaka 79
Mousseline Sauce 31
  Rich 32
Mr Michael Kelly's Sauce 58
Mrs Raffald's Traditional Orange
  Sauce 103
Mushroom Sauce 25, 27, 54
Mustard
  Mayonnaise 34
  Poppy Seed Sauce, Honey, and
    66
  Sauce 29
  Sauce, Mild 31
  Sauce, Papaya 68–9

Mutton
  Oyster Sauce for Roast Shoulder of
    43
  Sauce for Roast Shoulder of,
    without Oysters 43
My Grandmother's Suet Pastry 48

New Zealand Sauces 89
Ngo Pa Tsup 72
Noir, Beurre 29
Noisette, Beurre 29
Normandy Sauce 27
Nut Sauce 73
  Pine 93

Old English Game Sauce 47
Old-fashioned English Butterscotch
  Sauce 102
Olive Sauce 91, 93
Onion Sauce 25
  Brown 46
Onions, Liver, Bacon and, with
  Brown Onion Sauce 46
Op Tsup 72
Orange
  Coconut Sauce, Lemon Grass,
    and 65
  Green Peppercorn Vinegar, and
    15
  Marmalade and Wine Sauce,
    Quick 103
  Sauce, Mrs Raffald's Traditional
    103
  Sauce, Quick Apricot and 104
Ox Tongue, Fresh, with Raisin Sauce
  78
Oyster Sauce 61
  Millionaires' 61
  Roast Shoulder of Mutton, for 43

Pacific
  Pineapple Sauce 62
  Prawn Sauce 62
Paloise, Sauce 33
Papaya
  Mustard Sauce 68–9
  Sauce 68
  Sauce, Mango and 68
Paprika Sauce, Veal Cutlets with 81
Paradise
  Island Sauce, Carib 63
  Sauce 63

Parisienne, Sauce 27
Parsley
    Butter 30
    Butter Sauce, and 28–9
    Sauce 25
Peach Cream Sauce, Sherry and
    105
Peanut Sauce, Prawns with 88
Pears in a Wild Mint Vinaigrette
    84
Pepper Sauce 37–8, 39
Peppercorn
    Sauce, Port and Pink 73
    Vinegar, Lemon and Black 15
    Vinegar, Orange and Green 15
Perfect Gravy 44–5
Périgueux, Sauce 77
Pesto Sauce 87
Pigeon Sauce 43
Pine Nut Sauce 93
Pineapple Sauce
    Pacific 62
    Sweet and Sour 69
Pink Peppercorn Sauce, Port and 73
Piquante, Sauce 38
Pizzaiola, Salsa 91
Polonaise, Sauce 29
Poppy Seed Sauce, Honey, Mustard
    and 66
Pork
    Curry 94
    Goslings, Chicken, Lamb or Kid,
        Sauce for 43
    Loin of, Sauce for 91
Port
    Pink Peppercorn Sauce, and 73
    Wine Sauce 106
Portuguese
    Sauces 90–91
    Style, Loin of Veal 90
Poulette, Sauce 54
Prawn Sauce, Pacific 62
Prawns with Peanut Sauce 88
Prune Sauce 63

Quail Pudding, Rosa's 48
Quick
    Apricot and Orange Sauce 104
    Chicken, Hunters' Style 36
    Chocolate Sauce 100
    Orange Marmalade and Wine
        Sauce 103

Sweet Almond Sauce 99
Sweet Chocolate Sauce 99
Sweet Coffee Sauce 99
Sweet Ginger Sauce 99
Sweet Liqueur Sauce 99
Sweet Rum and Raisin Sauce
    99
Sweet White Sauce 99

Raisin Sauce
    Fresh Ox Tongue with 78
    Quick Sweet Rum and 99
Raspberry Vinegar 15
Ravigote, Sauce 27
Red
    Sauce, Canary Island 93
    Wine Demi-glace Sauce 35
Redcurrant Sauce 55
Reform Sauce 55
Rémoulade Sauce 340
Rich
    Caramel Sauce 102
    Cheese Sauce 25–6
    Cheese Sauce, Italian 26
    Madeira Sauce 35
    Mousseline Sauce 32
Riche, Sauce 27
Roast
    Beef Sauce 53
    Shoulder of Mutton, Oyster Sauce
        for 43
    Shoulder of Mutton, Sauce for,
        without Oysters 43
Robert Sauce 56
    Beauvilliers' Receipt for 57
Roeselare, Sauce, Francis Carroll
    Style 67
Rosa's Quail Pudding 48
Rose Petal
    Honey Sauce for Wild Breast of
        Duckling, and 73
    Vinegar 16
Rossini
    Sauce 77
    Steak 77
Roux 23
Royal Lamb Korma 74
Rum
    Custard Sauce 100
    Raisin Sauce, Quick Sweet, and 99
    Sauce 105
Russian Sauce 34

Sabayon Sauce 101
Salsa Pizzaiola 91
Salmon, Mock Smoked 18
San Francisco Barbecue Sauce 64
Sas, Dill 92
Sauce
    Allemande 27
    Any Land Fowl, Game or Turkey,
        for 43
    Bigarade 39
    Bourguignonne 40
    Cevettes, aux 54
    Charcutière 56
    Choron 33
    Colbert 87
    Czardas 86
    Diane 38
    Fayot 33
    Françoise 86
    Gibier 76
    Italienne 86
    Loin of Pork, for 91
    Louis 34
    Paloise 33
    Parisienne 27
    Périgueux 77
    Piquante 38
    Polonaise 29
    Pork, Goslings, Chicken, Lamb or
        Kid, for 43
    Poulette 54
    Ravigote 27
    Rémoulade 34
    Riche 27
    Roast Shoulder of Mutton without
        Oysters, for 43
    Robert, Beauvilliers' Receipt for 57
    Roeselare, Francis Carroll Style 67
    Rossini 77
    Stewed or Bouilli Beef, for 58
    Talleyrande 27
    Tripe or Cow-heel or Calf's Head,
        for 58
    Vierge 76
Savoury and Herb Butters 30
Scandinavian Sauces 92
Shallot Sauce 25
Sherry
    Peach Cream Sauce, and 105
    Sauce 105
    Sauce, Californian 60

Shrimp
  Butter 30
  Sauce 26
  Sauce, American 54
Skorthalia 80
Sofrito Sauce 69
Sour Cream and Dill Dip 97
Spanish Sauces 93
Steak Rossini 77
Stewed or Bouilli Beef, Sauce for 58
Stilton Sauce 74
Stocks 19–22
Strawberry-lemon Sauce 108
Suet Pastry, My Grandmother's 48
Sultana Sauce 51
Suzette Sauce 104
Sweet
  Almond Sauce, Quick 99
  Chocolate Sauce, Quick 99
  Coffee Sauce, Quick 99
  Ginger Sauce, Quick 99
  Liqueur Sauce, Quick 99
  Puddings, Eliza Acton's Wine Sauce for 106
  Rum and Raisin Sauce, Quick 99
  White Sauce, Quick 99
Sweet and Sour
  Pineapple Sauce 69
  Sauce 62
Swiss Fondue Sauce, Luxury 96

Talleyrande, Sauce 27
Tarragon Sauce, Lemon and 90
Tartare Sauce 57
Texas Tomato Sauce 59
Thai Sauces 94
Toffee Sauce, Icky Sticky Toffee Sponge with 102
Tomato
  Beef Sauce, and 86
  Garlic Dressing, and 97
  Green, Sauce, Hot and Spicy 61
  Honey and Lemon Dressing 97
  Sauce 45, 87
  Sauce, All-American 59
  Sauce, Texas 59
  Wine Sauce, Hake with Fresh Herb, and 65
Tom's Brittany Sauce Vinaigrette 18
Traditional
  Custard Sauce 100
  English Sauces 49–58
Tripe or Cow-heel or Calf's Head, Sauce for 58
Tromp's Lobster Butter 30
Truffle Sauces 77

Veal
  Cutlets with Paprika Sauce 81
  Loin of, Portuguese Style 90
  Stock 21
Vegetable Stock 22
Velouté Sauce 26

Very Good Irish Sauce, A 83
Vierge, Sauce 76
Vinaigrette
  Pears in a Wild Mint 84
  Tom's Brittany Sauce 17
Vinegars 14–16

Watercress Butter 30
Whisky Custard Sauce 100
White
  Fish Sauce 26
  Roux 23
  Sauce 25
  Sauce, Quick Sweet 99
  Wine, Honey and Garlic Marinade . . . and Sauce 64
Wine
  Demi-glace Sauce, Red 35
  Sauce for Sweet Puddings, Eliza Acton's 106
  Sauce, Hake with Fresh Herb, Tomato and 65
  Sauce, Port 106
  Sauce, Quick Orange Marmalade and 103
  Sauces 40
  White, Honey and Garlic Marinade . . . and Sauce 64
Worcestershire Sauce 44
Wow-wow Sauce 58

Your Own Favourite Liqueur Sauce 106